Enjoying the Active Life
After Fifty

Distributed by:

THE STEPHEN GREENE PRESS, INC.
Box 1000
Brattleboro, Vermont 05301

Enjoying the Active Life After Fifty

RALPH H. HOPP

STONE WALL PRESS, INC.
5 Byron Street
Boston, Massachusetts 02108

CREDITS

Cover. F.B. Grunzweig. *Chapter 3.* p. 17. Courtesy National Council on the Aging, Inc. p. 20. Courtesy Appalachian Mountain Club, George Bellerose Collection. p. 22. Courtesy National Council on the Aging, Inc. *Chapter 4.* p. 26. Courtesy Massachusetts Division of Fisheries & Game (Bill Byrne). p.31. Courtesy National Park Service (M. W. Williams). *Chapter 5.* pp. 35 and 37. Author's photos. *Chapter 6.* p. 39. Harriet W. Riggs. *Chapter 7.* p. 48. Courtesy Massachusetts Division of Fisheries & Game (Bill Byrne). p. 53. Courtesy Massachusetts Division of Fisheries & Game. *Chapter 8.* p. 58. Courtesy Massachusetts Division of Fisheries & Game. p. 61. Courtesy National Park Service (Jack Boucher). pp. 62 and 66. Courtesy The Orvis Company, Inc. p. 68. Courtesy National Park Service (M. W. Williams). p. 69. Courtesy National Park Service (Jack Boucher). *Chapter 9.* p. 72. Courtesy Mike Davis. *Chapter 10.* p. 78. F. B. Grunzweig. pp. 82 and 84. Courtesy Starcraft Company, Inc. *Chapter 11.* p. 88. Courtesy Appalachian Mountain Club (John T. Urban). p. 92. Courtesy National Park Service (M. W. Williams). p. 95. Courtesy Appalachian Mountain Club, George Bellerose Collection. p. 98. Courtesy Appalachian Mountain Club. p. 101. Courtesy Sawyer Canoe Company, Inc. *Chapter 12.* p. 104. Courtesy Community Boating, Inc., Boston. p. 107. Courtesy Appalachian Mountain Club, George Bellerose Collection. pp. 108 and 110. Courtesy Community Boating Inc., Boston. *Chapter 13.* p. 114. Courtesy Anita W. Brewer/Boston Area Bicycle Coalition. p. 118. Courtesy National Council on the Aging, Inc. *Chapter 14.* p. 122. Courtesy Natick Racquet Club. p. 128. Courtesy Seabrook Island Company, Grand Masters Tournament (Charleston, S. C.). *Chapter 15.* pp. 130, 133 and 136. Joeanne D. McGrail. *Chapter 16.* p. 140. Karen R. Preuss. *Chapter 17.* pp. 146, 148 and 150. Courtesy Appalachian Mountain Club, George Bellerose Collection. p. 153. Courtesy National Park Service (M. W. Williams). *Chapter 18.* p. 155. Author's photo. p. 160. F. B. Grunzweig. *Chapter 19.* p. 163. Courtesy National Park Service (Richard Frear). p. 167. Courtesy Vail Associates, Inc. (Peter Runyon). p. 170. Courtesy Swiss National Tourist Office. *Chapter 20.* p. 173. Courtesy Vail Associates, Inc. (Peter Runyon). p. 176. Killington Ski Area, courtesy Boston Ski & Sports Club. p. 179. Courtesy Boston Ski & Sports Club.

Copyright © 1979 by STONE WALL PRESS, Inc.

LIBRARY OF CONGRESS CATALOGING IN PUBLICATION DATA

Hopp, Ralph Harvey, 1915-
    Enjoying the active life after fifty.

    Includes bibliographies.
    1. Aged—Recreation.   2. Outdoor recreation.
I. Title.
GV185.H66   790.19'4   79-10599
ISBN 0-913276-26-X

First printing June 1979

Contents

EDITOR'S NOTE

The chapters in this book have been arranged to introduce you to the gentlest, least vigorous outdoor activities first, and then proceed to more vigorous, technical activities. The swimming chapter precedes the water sports chapters for obvious safety reasons. While you may wish to skip to vigorous activities that may interest you, we caution you to make sure that your body is physically prepared—either through an exercise program or by frequent participation in the outdoor activities described earlier in the book. A stress test from your physician is also recommended.

Foreword

IT IS NOW widely recognized that many health problems which have traditionally been ascribed to aging are in actuality due to associated physical inactivity. Inactivity has been convincingly linked to premature deterioration of cardiorespiratory capacity, loss of muscular strength and tone, thinning of bones (*osteoporosis*), decreased joint flexibility, and development of metabolic disorders of lipid (fat) and carbohydrate metabolism. These conditions in turn are major causes of reduced vigor and work capacity and chronic fatigue; low back pain; immobility; brittle, easily fractured bones; obesity; diabetes mellitus; coronary heart disease; and premature death. In addition, a lack of regular exercise and fitness appears to contribute to nervous tension and depression.

In contrast, regular endurance-type (aerobic) exercise, involving rhythmic movements of large muscle groups (e.g., walking, jogging, biking), offers a rewarding way of improving the quality and perhaps length of life. This is accomplished through reducing the above-mentioned premature aging processes and degenerative diseases; increasing cardiorespiratory capacity and efficiency; improving mobility, flexibility, and muscular tone and bone strength; and reducing body fat. There are other positive effects—increasing vigor, self-confidence, and health consciousness, and improving the ability to handle stress.

The following guidelines should be helpful to middle-aged and older people for establishing a life-long plan of regular, safe exercise:

1. Have a thorough medical evaluation, preferably by a physician who is an active exerciser him- or herself, to detect possible contraindications to strenuous exercise or special precautions which should be taken. This evaluation should include an exercise electrocardiogram test to detect possible dangers from hidden (latent) coronary artery disease, and to determine your relative physical fitness level as an aid in selecting a conditioning activity or activities within safe limits.

2. Make exercise a regular part of your daily routine. If you can't do it daily, a minimum investment required to produce physiological benefits is thirty minutes three times a week. Also, take every opportunity you possibly can to walk more. Remember that those who can't find time for exercise will have to find time for sickness and disability.

3. Don't think of fitness as a crash program. Start slowly and gradually increase the duration, frequency, and intensity of exercise within prescribed limits. Also take time to warm up with stretching and low intensity exercises and follow the workout with a cooling down period. These precautions will help reduce the risk of musculoskeletal injury and cardiovascular complications.

4. Some exertion and breathlessness is necessary in order to achieve the cardiovascular, metabolic, and psychological benefits of exercise. This is part of living life to the fullest.

5. Find an activity or activities which you enjoy and can get involved in. Exercise is also more likely to become part of your lifestyle if it is done out-of-doors in a pleasant environment with companions you enjoy. Also, try to avoid competition with yourself or others, which can spoil the enjoyment of the experience. In addition, competition can produce mental stress and cause an individual to exceed safe, sensible limits.

This book, by Ralph Hopp, himself a life-long exercise enthusiast, will provide the reader with basic, practical information and references for beginning a wide variety of aerobic sports and recreational activities. These activities will fill leisure hours for older people in a positive way that improves physical health and emotional well-being.

ARTHUR S. LEON, M.D.
Associate Professor
Laboratory of Physiological Hygiene
School of Public Health
  and the Department of Medicine
University of Minnesota
Minneapolis, Minnesota

Preface

THE EXPRESSION, "Life begins at 40," had always seemed to me to be an exaggeration of the truth, simply an attempt to assuage the trauma of aging. When, eventually, I reached that magic age, I found there was, indeed, validity to the assertion. Some may feel that to suggest fun and fitness after 50 likewise is fanciful. I disagree. This book is designed to guide the reader to activities that will bring about significant changes in the quality of his or her life, even though one has passed the age of 50. There is no reason why most people cannot have both fun and fitness, whether 50, or 70, or older.

As we get older we often have to work a little harder at having fun. If we have not cultivated the art of enjoying life, we may have to overcome some ingrained bad habits. But the situation is far from hopeless. There are innumerable examples we read about every day—some included in this book—of people well past their allotted three score and ten who have found great delight in some new activity. We all know about Grandma Moses, of course. But have you heard of E. E. Tutor of Jackson, Mississippi? He started jogging at 77 and now, at more than 80, jogs 2 miles daily. Lowell Thomas, well into his 80's, is an ardent skier. They are having fun, and feeling fit in the bargain.

Why is it that some people at 60 appear old, while others maintain their youthful appearance? Perhaps it is an inherited characteristic. But psychologists claim we are products of our environment. The truth probably lies somewhat in both camps. Not that we have to strive to stay young forever. That is not the objective. What we want is to enjoy life, and health, whatever our age. As Mrs. Brice said, in *Funny Girl*, "I don't want to be young. I did that already."

Our frame of mind has a great influence on how we feel, how we react, how we age, how we look. We have control over our moods. They are the outgrowths of such influences as physical activity, health, interests, enjoyments, food, habits, our work, and our friends. Most of these we can do something about. Enjoying oneself through outdoor recreation is a very positive step toward improving one's outlook.

This book is not about aging. But there are many suggestions in it on how to adjust to it, slow it down. It is not about retirement, although it very well could be a guide to retirement activities. It is not a book on physical fitness. Nevertheless, if you follow the activities described in it you will go a long way toward maintaining fitness. The underlying message it conveys is that the development and maintenance of a healthy attitude toward life as one grows older can be achieved in large measure by continued participation in pursuits that will tend to keep one younger and optimistic.

The activities I have chosen are fairly selective. Mostly they are the ones in which my wife and I regularly participate. Some we didn't start until after we were 50 years old. All are outside activities. A few will require physical exertion and should be followed only after checking with your doctor. Others are mild forms of recreation, such as walking or birdwatching. Almost anyone can participate in the majority of them.

Much credit for the idea of this book must go to my wife, Dorothy. She came late to many of these sports, and has inspired our friends and relatives with her enthusiasm and ability to participate competently, despite her age. She also provided the inspiration for me to write this book. I have done so in the hopes that others past 50 also will be encouraged to enjoy such sports.

We were both in our mid-50's when we began downhill skiing. Many thought we were foolhardy. It was one of the greatest things we ever did. My wife took up waterskiing as she was approaching 60. She now slaloms and loves it! The same with tennis. We now play almost daily during the summer.

We have never felt better! We believe, and doctors' examinations bear this out, that we are in better physical condition now than anytime in the 37 years we have been married. Exercise and proper diet are the essential elements in our daily program. To call it a program is a slight exaggeration. We are not slavish joggers nor exercisers, but we do believe in doing some physical activity every day if possible, even if it is no more than climbing stairs rather than taking an elevator. We believe in following the active sports or hobbies that we enjoy, and our physical fitness is a by-product. Also, we believe in a philosophy of moderation in everything we do, whether eating, drinking, exercising, or working. It is essential to our well-being. Overindulgence is one of life's real hazards.

But the key element above all is *participation*. One has to remain active, physically and mentally. Growing old is more a state of mind than it is a physical change. We can attest to that. One does not have to act old just because one has reached 50 or 60.

People and their attitudes have changed over the years. Retirement used to be looked upon as a time when you could sit back, take it easy. The appealing thing about retirement today is that it frees you to *do* the things you haven't had time for while working. There may be some people who do not know what to do with themselves after they retire. This book is especially for them.

Don't be concerned about your lack of knowledge of any of the activities described. I have provided lists of books and magazines that will give you the information to get started. Also, don't fret about looking like a beginner. There are many beginners and few experts in any recreational sport. We do not pretend to excel in these activities, but we certainly have fun. And we are participating, not just watching. That's what is important.

Perhaps the reason I have chosen outside activities is that there is a special bonus involved—the enjoyment of the outdoors. We are blessed with a beautiful country. It has been my good fortune to have traveled considerably, both here and abroad. The United States has an extraordinary wealth of scenic beauty, matched by few other places in the world. Many of the sports included here take advantage of that beauty—alpine and cross-country skiing, boating, fishing, sailing, canoeing, backpacking, camping, hiking, birdwatching, and hunting. One cannot but be concerned that these beauties may not be preserved for the enjoyment of future generations.

The Isaak Walton League, founded in 1922, for example, represents one of many conservation groups dedicated to the preservation of outdoor America. The Sierra Club and the National Audubon Society also serve as watchdogs on behalf of the public, advocating the proper management of our natural environment. They take within their purview the preservation of our fields, streams and lakes, the development of parks and recreation areas, and the prevention of wildlife destruction by selfish interests. These organizations encourage scientific research in conservation techniques and the passing of laws and regulations to prevent the depletion of our outdoor resources. Above all these organizations have stimulated a national movement of concerned citizens who speak out on behalf of nature and the values to be gained from its enjoyment.

It is your country, your land, your life. Enjoy them!

Ralph H. Hopp

1   *The Best Years of Our Lives*

"The sun setting is no less beautiful than the sun rising."
Paul Green

THERE HAS been precious little written that is optimistic about growing old. It is only in recent years that we have begun to recognize that "growing old" has been a cultural expectation. Anyone over 50 simply was expected to follow the "normal" pattern. Fortunately, evidence is building that the maturing process in humans, as in fruits, results in something sweet and mellow, something to be savored. More and more of us can agree with Walter B. Pitkin, who some 30 years ago, wrote in his book, *The Best Years*, that the latter phase of one's life is the time to live with zest, not for a day or two, but for years and years. The best years come after 50, he said. I believe he was right.

There is a semantic problem in talking about people over 50. The sociologists, psychologists, and others writing on aging, are struggling with terms that refer to this group. Reference is made to "seniors," "older Americans," "the elderly," "the old," "the oldsters," "the aged," "the older adult," "the matured," "the age of integrity," and other such euphemisms. I prefer to deal directly with age groups, and thus the title of this book speaks to those "over 50." These people, to be sure, are in a later phase of their lives, and thus are "older," but that does not make them "old" in the usual meaning of the term.

E. B. Palmore, in his book, *Normal Aging*, reports on the studies made by the Duke University Center for the Study of Aging and Human Development. The results by and large disprove many of the myths about growing old. Some of the popular misconceptions include the belief that with advancing age goes a decline in intelligence, that one is more prone to illness, there is a much slower reaction time, and sex life is nil. Other factors, such as socio-economic status and level of intelligence, appear to have more effect on many of these characteristics than does aging.

It is also untrue that older people by and large are unhappy, or that they dwell on the past. Dr. Bernice L. Neugarten of the University of Chicago found that in her research the majority of older people said the present was the best time of their lives.

With 1 out of 10 people in the U.S. over 65 today, and 1 in 5 anticipated by the year 2000, there is increasing attention given to utilizing the creative potential of this growing group. These individuals have a rich background of experience, more free unscheduled time, and 2/3 of them are in good physical condition. Well over 20 million people in the U.S. are over 65, constituting a vital national resource. It is not a segment of our population that needs "to be taken care of" as much as one that should be *utilized*.

One of the encouraging findings in medical studies is that our physical condition, as we grow older, does not deteriorate so much from aging as it does from inactivity. And, fortunately, it is a reversible condition. For many who have been leading increasingly sedentary lives, and thus have arrived at a deconditioned state, it is possible to regain much of their former verve through a program of physical activity. Such a program doesn't have to be costly, boring, or require a great deal of effort. In fact, enjoying some of the activities described in this book, offers improved physical condition as an important by-product.

Elliot Carlson, in an article in a recent issue of *Dynamic Maturity*, wrote that boredom is a serious disease today, anguishing millions. He claims that doctors' offices fill up with people who have nothing really wrong with them except boredom, even though they may have many symptoms of illnesses of various kinds. One way, he suggests, to alleviate the pain of boredom is to engage in such physical activity as jogging, tennis, and other participative sports. Not only will such sports relieve the boredom and tone up the body, they will put excitement in your life.

Dr. Alex Comfort, author of the recent book *The Good Age*, put in writing what most of us apparently feel. He said that aging has no effect on you as a person. "When you are 'old' you will feel no different and be no different from what you are now or were when you were young, except that more experiences will have happened. Older people are in fact young people inhabiting old bodies." Many times I have heard it said by my friends that they feel themselves to be no older than they were many years earlier. Their appearances change, of course, but "inside" they feel the same. Our needs and attitudes, desires, and the things that satisfy them will not change with passing years. Remaining physically active can play a dominant role in retaining the attributes of youth. The physical changes of aging inevitably will take place, but it is within your power to slow them down. There is no end to personal testimony, and this is substantiated by mounting medical evidence, that physical activity is the enemy of the aging process.

For some their 50th birthday marks a mental turning point in their lives. For others this crucial point may be at some other significant birthday, even as early as 40. The experience may border on the traumatic, if they have fallen prey to the role society has laid out for them. They are about to live up to its expectations. How sad! These benchmarks can and should signal the beginning of a period in which life can become richer. Instead of catering to society's tradition, it is better to believe with Bernard Baruch, who said, "I'll never be an old man. To me old age is always 15 years older than I am."

There is no doubt that, physiologically, there is some decline in physical fitness as one grows older. That decline is not limited, however, to "old" people. Boxers, football and basketball players, and other professional athletes reach a high point early in life, after which they also decline. It is claimed that middle age for the average American male begins at 28. It is the aging process, still not understood for the most part, that causes change. And it is a continuum, not a change suddenly marked by a birthday. Barring illness or accident, most people can remain functional in nearly all ways almost to the time of death. The degree to which they continue to function depends in large part on them, their attitudes, and perhaps their socioeconomic status. Certainly one important factor is the extent to which they remain physically active.

Early retirement, either by choice or by company or institutional policy, has become an issue of considerable interest to many who are studying the effects of aging. With the improved health and economic status of those retiring, we have essentially developed a leisure class. The recreational and travel industries, government planning groups, and social agencies are not fully prepared to cope with the growing numbers in this leisure group.

There are those who advocate, instead of leisure, continued work and responsibilities as best, especially for those who had pressures as leaders and executives during their working years. The Gray Panthers, a militant organization of older citizens, urges the abolition of mandatory retirement for those still willing and able to work. Others extoll the virtues of shedding the mantels of fixed schedules and pressures. They advocate enjoying the good life.

It comes down to individual cases. What is good for one is not necessarily the best for another. Largely, it depends upon how well one has prepared for the period of retirement. Preparation has to begin before, much before, the last year of working. The adoption of a personal philosophy toward leisure, toward the enjoyment of life, and toward such matters as the proper use of vacation time, early in your career—these will have a profound effect on how you cope with retirement. As Pitkin said, "Your best way to avoid the horrors of second childhood is to keep your first childhood alive and lusty." If you thrilled at getting a new wagon at 10, you can still thrill at getting a new motorcycle at 60. And don't be too sophisticated to show it. Let it all "hang out" and your enthusiasm will be contagious.

Although much more planning and program development remains to be accomplished for those over 50, there is considerable activity, even today, that focuses on senior citizens. Most colleges and universities offer courses at little or no cost for those over a certain age. Municipal and state agencies have programs. Some churches and social groups are developing activities. Information on such programs can be obtained at your public library, in the telephone book yellow pages, probably under "senior citizens," or even from the governor's office. Don't be put off. Insist on getting information. Listed below are some publications you may want to look at or purchase, which will provide leads as well as interesting reading. Many programs are supported by your taxes. If you don't take advantage of them you are being short-changed.

More information undoubtedly will flow from grant funds provided by the U.S. Administration on Aging, which has recently received a record $400 million from Congress. It supports the development of model programs of physical fitness activities for older Americans. The goal is to motivate groups, such as community agencies, YM-YWCA organizations, and others, to provide leadership and facilities to implement these programs for those over 60.

The National Association for Human Development, also with funds from the Administration on Aging, recently conducted a pilot project to train physical fitness leaders for the elderly. It furthers the goal of the Older Americans Act, which is to "encourage the development of services designed to enable older Americans to attain and maintain physical and mental well-being through programs of regular physical activity and exercise." Also, the National Institute on Aging is undertaking a vigorous program of research in all aspects of aging.

As the song says, "There must be more to life than growing old."

RECOMMENDED READING

Books:

Comfort, Alex. *A Good Age.* New York, Crown, 1976. $5.95.
An interesting book by an authority on aging. Presents his material in the form of subject entries, like an encyclopedia. Includes quotations from outstanding people on the subject of aging. Also describes, in vignette form, activities of well-known older people who have remained active despite their age. All in all, a witty, persuasive book.

Popov, Ivan. *Stay Young.* New York, Grosset & Dunlap, 1976. $1.95.

Stonecypher, Dr. D. D., Jr. *Getting Older and Staying Young; A Doctor's Prescription for Continuing Vitality in Later Life.* New York, Norton, 1974. $8.95.
Dispels the myths surrounding old age. Prescribes counteractions to physical and psychological aging, advocating using capacities to the fullest to preserve them.

Successful Aging; A Conference Report. Durham, N.C., Duke University Center for the Study of Aging and Human Development, 1974.

Taylor, Dr. Robert B. *Feeling Alive After 65; The Complete Medical Guide for Senior Citizens and Their Families.* New Rochelle, N.Y., Arlington House, 1973. $8.95.

Magazines:

Aging. 10 issues per year. Superintendent of Documents, U.S. Government Printing Office, Washington, D.C. 20402. $5.05 per year.

Filled with news of developments throughout the country in programs, legislation, new agencies concerned with aging, people working with senior citizens, and examples of older people participating in various activities.

Dynamic Maturity. Bi-monthly. Action for Independent Maturity, American Association of Retired Persons, 1909 K Street NW, Washington, D.C. 20049. Annual dues: $3.00 per year.

Designed to enrich the middle, pre-retirement years. The magazine is available to anyone over 50 who joins AIM. Membership applications should be sent to AIM, Membership Processing Department, P.O. Box 199, Long Beach, Ca. 90801.

Modern Maturity. Bi-monthly. American Association of Retired Persons, 1909 K Street NW, Washington, D.C. 20049. Annual dues: $3.00 per year.

One of the real bargains! Magazine is beautifully illustrated, more than worth the membership cost. Other membership perquisites are a bonus. Membership available to anyone 55 or older.

Retirement Living. 10 issues per year. 150 East 58th Street, New York 10022. $7.95 per year.

For those retired or planning their retirement. Included are articles on physical activities, such as "Time for Active Sports," "Tennis: Fun at 60," "Tips for the Over-55 Skier," "Not Ready for the Rocking Chair," "Bragging His Way to Fitness at 94," "You're Only as Young as You Field: Kids and Kubs League for Ages 75 and Up."

2 *Benefits of Physical Activity*

NUMEROUS CULT-LIKE activities have emerged in recent years, each promising significant beneficial results to its practitioners. Whether it is yoga, isometrics, transcendental meditation, or jogging, the benefits to be gained from such activities depend in large part on the motivation people bring to them. Joining a health club, for example, is in itself an act signifying an individual's concern with his or her physical condition. It already implies a willingness to make a commitment for improvement.

Doing something is an important first step. Too often, however, these commitments are of limited duration. Human nature takes over. Regular exercise undertaken simply as a commitment for self-improvement tends to be somewhat boring. Unexpired health club memberships, as a consequence, can be purchased by watching your daily paper's want ads. Too bad! Exercise really is good for us. And it doesn't have to be boring, or expensive. There are many ways in which we can enjoy ourselves while exercising, and often with little cost.

Not everyone, of course, is bored with jogging or calisthenics or yoga. They can be appealing, especially when one becomes fascinated with the change taking place in one's physical condition and mental well-being. The day you notice more spring in your step, more energy, less tension and anxiety, improved sexual response, or more optimism, there sets in an incentive factor and enthusiasm for the exercising that before had seemed just hard work. For example, Hayden Gilmore, in his book *Jog for Your Life*, describes his addiction to jogging and, in exaggerated lyrical hyperbole, tries to tell the whole world of the great benefits he has experienced from it.

Do exercise and physical activity improve the health? Are there psychological benefits to be gained from a regimen of running or swimming or cycling? Almost everyone who has studied the effects of exercise believes that the answer to both questions is "yes." The American Heart Association states that "regular, vigorous exercise enhances the quality of life by increasing the physical capability for work and play."

If one embarks upon an exercise program for the sake of physical and psychological improvement, it is important to take certain precautions. Medical authorities advise anyone over 35 to take a "stress test" to determine the maximum exercise limits to be observed. Especially for sedentary individuals there are serious risks in launching into a program of strenuous exercise. Such activities as jogging, social or competitive tennis, rapid cross-country skiing, or any activity which requires continuous high-level exertion, bursts of energy, or sustained endurance, should be undertaken only after medical approval. This is especially advisable for middle-aged men, but also for older men and women.

The improvement of one's physical and mental condition is, of course, sufficient reason in itself to engage in exercise. But there is no reason why one shouldn't have fun in the process. The benefits of exercise can be gained as well from recreational games and sports if they are done on a regular, continuous basis. Such participation also should be preceded by some physical conditioning program. Often a slight adjustment in daily activities can provide such conditioning. Walking instead of driving. Climbing stairs instead of using the elevator. Reduction in the amount of smoking. Avoidance of overeating. Proper diet. All these contribute to a conditioning of the body. Such preconditioning activities are valuable in their own right even if one did not pursue more strenuous sports.

It is surprising then, if exercising is so good for us, that so few older people take advantage of its benefits. Partly it is lack of knowledge of the importance of exercising in maintaining physical and mental health. Recently, it was reported by the National Adult Physical Fitness Survey that only 39 percent of Americans 60 and older get any systematic exercise. The favorite form of exercise is walking. Only 1 percent are joggers, 6 percent do calisthenics, 3 percent ride bicycles, and 4 percent swim. Yet, according to C. Carson Conrad of the President's Council on Physical Fitness and Sports, by far the greater majority believe they get all the exercise they need. Surely it is a rife blissful ignorance!

With the considerable attention being given to the issues surrounding older Americans, particularly at the national level, we can expect an improvement in participation. The Older Americans Act, the Administration on Aging, the National Association for Human Development, and many other groups, are working to inform, motivate, and enlist the support and participation of older persons in physical activities.

Dr. Kenneth H. Cooper, author or co-author of the popular books on aerobics, has extensive clinical data from working with U.S. Air Force personnel, mostly under the age of 50. He found that regular exercising contributes to the body's capacity to absorb oxygen. Oxygen, which is not stored in the body, is necessary to fully utilize the food we eat. This in turn produces the energy we need for work or play. Our fitness is measured by our ability to absorb the quantity of oxygen required for whatever activity we undertake. If we are consistently inactive, our body has adapted to a low oxygen requirement. Should we be called upon to exceed our normal activity, our body can't hack it. Dr. Cooper has devised a point system with which we can measure our fitness. You are given several choices of exercises. By selecting one or more of these, you can devise a program that will gradually bring you up to a fit condition.

The reason you huff and puff when you run is that your body is trying to get more oxygen into your system to burn the food to provide the energy needed for that level of exercise. "Your heart is pounding," says Dr. Cooper, "as it tries to pump more blood (which carries the oxygen) around the body. And the blood is racing through the blood vessels to every extremity as it tries to deliver more oxygen." Inactivity simply hastens the deterioration of the body, reducing its capacity to deliver oxygen, resulting in the resigned declaration that "I guess I'm getting old."

In some stress tests physicians measure the maximum oxygen uptake, or aerobic capacity, which is a measure of fitness. This capacity decreases with advancing age, disease, or when one is out of condition. With proper exercise older people can increase this capacity until it is at a level normally attributed to much younger people. A study recently completed in England examined a group with an average age of 60, who pursued an extensive program of exercises for 10 years. During that decade they progressively improved their performance until, at 70, they were physiologically more fit than they had been 10 years earlier. Some of the decrease in work or play capacity, obviously, is caused not so much by age as it is by physical inactivity. Fortunately, even though an older person in otherwise normal health has arrived at a deconditioned state, it generally is possible to regain an improved condition. "To rest is to rust," says Paul Bragg, a 94-year old leader of daily exercise programs in Hawaii. "Old age," he claims, "is just an excuse laggards use to cover up bad habits."

Dr. Arthur S. Leon of the University of Minnesota Laboratory of Physiological Hygiene, has analyzed the effects of exercise, with particular reference to coronary heart disease. He has found that there is clear evidence that regular exercise reduces the demands made on the heart. The heart rate is reduced usually after several weeks of exercising. And the mortality rate for victims of coronary heart disease is known to be less among people with slower heart beats. Unfortunately, the discontinuation of exercising results in the heart returning rapidly to its faster pace.

A low aerobic capacity, it has been found, leads to fatigue, reduced capacity for work or play, reduced pulmonary function, an increased heart rate, a decrease in circulating blood volume, muscle wasting, and obesity. Physically active people have been shown to have lower blood pressure and less frequent hypertension than comparable sedentary individuals. And there is a significant correlation between high blood pressure and the incidence of coronary heart disease.

Studies have shown that an improved tolerance to emotional stress does occur with regular exercise. Physical activity is essential for mental health and is emotionally therapeutic, according to Dr. Greenspan of the Menninger Clinic. The World Health Organization defines health as "physical, mental, and social well-being, not merely the absence of disease or infirmity." Since physical fitness is a component of good health, such activities as walking, running, cycling, cross-country skiing, or swimming add significantly to the quality of life.

The effects of exercise on the life span of humans has yet to be determined experimentally. Existing data so far appears inconclusive. On the other hand, experiments on the effects of life-long exercise on albino rats demonstrated that exercised rats lived 25 percent longer than their non-exercised counterparts. Dr. Irene Gore, University of London, who studies the biological effects of aging, affirms that getting old is a state of mind. Machines wear out from use, but human bodies thrive on it. Such declines as are experienced with age are usually due not to years, but to disease, mental and physical inactivity, and just plain laziness.

Dr. Alexander Leaf, in a report in a recent *Scientific American*, analyzed the life styles of several isolated populations in the world where long, vigorous, disease-free life is the rule. He concluded that diet and exercise are primary causes of longevity in the three cultures studied. As one researcher stated, while it is not presently possible to determine from existing data whether habitual life-long exercise adds years to life, it appears certain that it adds *life to years*.

CHOICE OF EXERCISE.   Assuming a normal, healthy physical condition, how much and what kind of exercise should one engage in? It is largely a matter of personal interest. For some it may be gardening. Some may prefer indoor calisthenics. Recreational enjoyment plays a vital part in my choice of physical activity. Also, I prefer out-of-doors activity, winter and summer, since fresh air and an often pleasant environment are an important part of the enjoyment. Skiing in the Colorado mountains. Canoeing in the Quetico–Superior National Forest. Fishing in the lakes of the "Land of sky blue waters" or the Canadian wilderness. Tennis in the park. Horseback riding among the Egyptian pyramids. Motorcycling in the Wisconsin countryside. Sailing on a sunshiny day with soft breezes and billowy clouds. These are my choices.

One of the facts to be faced in winter months by those who live in the northern tier of states is that outdoor preconditioning and exercising activities must, of necessity, be limited. There are substitutes for those who prefer to remain indoors. Among these are running in place, swimming, jumping rope, or many of the exercise opportunities available at your local YW–YMCA or Jewish community center. Deliberately climbing stairs faster than normal, and more than perhaps is required by the daily routine, assists in keeping one's legs in condition, particularly for such sports as alpine or cross-country skiing.

For sedentary individuals the beginning of an exercise program will commonly bring aching muscles, joints, and tendons. These effects tend to be transitory. Moderating the exercise, or temporarily discontinuing it, usually brings relief. Wearing proper shoes often will avoid many problems with feet or legs. Correct shoes are especially important for older people engaged in jogging or tennis, or even walking. Cheap canvas sneakers should be avoided.

A minimum of 30 minutes of vigorous physical activity per week is all that is necessary to offer some protection against coronary heart disease, according to Dr. J. N. Morris of the London School of Hygiene and Tropical Medicine. Brisk walking, cycling, or jogging 3 times a week for 20 to 30 minutes a session will bring about significant improvement in physical fitness. These improvements should be evident within 4 weeks. Certain precautions are advised. One should engage in brief warm-up and cool-down exercises before and after vigorous activity. Also doctors advise that such activities should be no sooner than 2 hours after a large meal. And very hot showers should be avoided immediately following strenuous exercise.

Table 1, compiled by Dr. S. M. Fox and colleagues, lists activities of differing intensities. This gradation should be helpful in choosing the activity at the specific level of exercise most appropriate for you, and according to your special interests.

TABLE 1

Occupational	*Recreational*
I	
Desk work; driving an auto; typing; electric calculating machine operation	Standing; walking 1 mph; flying; motorcycling; playing cards; sewing
II	
Auto repair; radio/TV repair; janitorial work; manual typing; bartending	Level walking 2 mph; level bicycling 5 mph; riding lawnmower; billiards; bowling; skeet; shuffleboard; light woodworking; driving power boat; golf with power cart; canoeing 2.5 mph; horseback riding at walk; playing piano and many other musical instruments

Occupational	Recreational
III	
Brick laying; plastering; pushing 45 kg. or 100 lb. load on wheelbarrow; machine assembly; driving trailer-truck in traffic; moderate load of welding; cleaning windows	Walking 3 mph; cycling 6 mph; pitching horseshoes; 6-man noncompetitive volleyball; golf, pulling bag cart; archery; small boat sailing; fly fishing while standing with waders; horseback, sitting to trot; badminton doubles, social; pushing light lawnmower; energetic musician
IV	
Painting masonry; paperhanging; light carpentry	Walking 3.5 mph; cycling 8 mph; table tennis; golf, carrying clubs; dancing foxtrot; badminton singles; tennis doubles; raking leaves; hoeing; many calisthenics
V	
Digging garden; shoveling light earth	Walking 4 mph; cycling 10 mph; canoeing 4 mph; horseback, posting to trot; stream fishing, walking in waders in light current; ice or roller-skating 9 mph
VI	
Shoveling 4½ kg. or 10 lbs., 10 loads per minute	Walking 5 mph; cycling 11 mph; competitive badminton; tennis singles; splitting wood; snow shoveling; mowing grass with push mower; square dancing; light downhill skiing; cross-country skiing 2.5 mph in loose snow; waterskiing
VII	
Digging ditches; carrying 36 kg. or 80 lbs.; sawing hardwood	Jogging 5 mph; cycling 12 mph; horseback at gallop; vigorous downhill skiing; basketball; mountain climbing; ice hockey; canoeing 5 mph; touch football; paddleball
VIII	
Shoveling 5½ kg. or 14 lbs., 10 loads per minute	Running 5.5 mph; cycling 13 mph; cross-country skiing 4 mph in loose snow; squash, social; social handball; fencing; vigorous basketball
IX	
Shoveling 7½+ kg. or 16+ lbs., 10 loads per minute	Running 6–10 mph; cross-country skiing 5+ mph in loose snow; competitive handball; competitive squash

Fox, S. M., J. P. Naughton, and P. A. Gorman. *Modern Concepts of Cardiovascular Disease*, v. 41, no. 6, pp. 25–30, June 1972. By permission of the American Heart Association, Inc.

Since the physical capacity for work is measured by oxygen uptake, Table 2, which lists oxygen requirements of different activities, is also a useful guide. It was compiled by the Colorado Heart Association.

TABLE 2. APPROXIMATE OXYGEN COST OF VARIOUS ACTIVITIES

Oxygen Cost (ml O_2 /min/kg body wt)	Activity
3.2	Sleeping
4.0	Sitting at ease
4.8	Standing at ease
9.0	Walking 2.0 mph
12.5	Walking 3.0 mph; housework; cycling 5.0 mph
16.0	Walking 4.0 mph on level; 2.0 mph at 10 percent grade
20.0	Walking 4.5 mph level; cycling 9.5 mph; gardening; manual labor; dancing rumba
24.0	Walking 5.0 mph level; 3.0 mph at 10 percent grade
29.0	Running 5.5 mph level; swimming breast stroke 40 yds/min; climbing stairs
31.4	Bicycling 13 mph
38.0	Running 7.0 mph; swimming the crawl 50 yds/min; heavy labor
48.0	Running 8.0 mph; climbing stairs with 30 lb. load
57.0	Running 10.0 mph; competitive cross-country running or skiing
68.5	All-out competitive running, skiing, rowing, swimming

American Heart Association, "Exercise Testing and Training of Apparently Healthy Individuals: A Handbook for Physicians." The Association, 1972, p. 24. © American Heart Association. Reprinted with permission.

This book has as its main objective the encouragement of those over 50 to remain physically active, and have fun in the bargain. Therefore, the activities I describe are all in that category of "fun," but they vary one from the other in the amount of physical exertion required for participation. All of them do not require enough activity to achieve fitness as described by Dr. Cooper and others concerned with health maintenance. A judicious combination of activities might bring this result. Fishing, by itself, will not develop physical endurance. But fishing and jogging or cycling might. *The*

New Aerobics, by Dr. Cooper, provides a useful guide for men for selecting activities, and *Aerobics for Women*, by Dr. Cooper and his wife, is helpful for women.

Whatever else you might be stimulated to do, by all means get out, have fun, and participate in some kind of activity. The dividends will exceed your expectations.

FOR FURTHER INFORMATION

Cooper, Dr. Kenneth H. *Aerobics.* New York, Evans, 1968. $6.95.

——. *The New Aerobics.* New York, Evans, 1970. $6.95.

——. *The Aerobic Way.* New York, Evans, 1977. $10.00.

Cooper, Mildred, and Kenneth H. Cooper. *Aerobics for Women.* New York, Evans, 1972. $6.95.

DeVries, Dr. Herbert A. *Vigor Regained.* Englewood Cliffs, N.J., Prentice-Hall, 1974.

Gore, Dr. Irene. *Add Years to Your Life and Life to Your Years.* New York, Stein and Day, 1975. $1.95.

3　　　　*Walking*

SOME 20 years ago, at a time when activity for the sake of fitness was virtually nonexistent, I began walking to my office each morning, a distance of over 2 miles. Coincidentally a cartoon appeared in our local paper which depicted two policemen in a patrol car watching a walker. The caption read: "He looks suspicious. Shall we pick him up?"

Fortunately, times have changed. Walking today has become an accepted form of exercise, shared by millions of people the world over. Medical experts have dubbed walking the nearly perfect exercise for improving physical and mental health. It is an ideal activity for older people and the claims of its benefits are persuasive.

Quite aside from the physical and mental benefits of walking, it can be pure pleasure. Like camping and some of the other activities described in this book, it is the unexpected dividends from walking which make it such a pleasurable activity. Bern Keating recently enumerated the joys he found in walking. Among the auxiliary interests he has developed are logging birds he has identified, observing the first crocuses, catching the first budding willows, or ripening fruit, photographing architectural discoveries, identifying edible mushrooms, window shopping, problem solving, zoo visiting, surprising wild animals, and recording on film many wonders of nature, common but mostly overlooked by our wheeled friends.

Walking, of course, is often simply a way of getting from one place to another, generally in a hurry to meet an appointment. Under such circumstances one has very little chance to contemplate the joy of walking. Rather it is deemed merely a slow mode of travel and often it is forsaken for the auto or the bus. The pleasure that comes from strolling, or even walking briskly as a means of achieving fitness, is quite another matter.

Americans have not developed the habit of walking to the same degree as Europeans. In Europe the evening stroll is an accepted practice, particularly on a nice Sunday evening. The streets are almost as crowded then as during the daytime when the shops are open. Anyone who has traveled in Europe will recall the number of people walking along roadways. Fortunately for them, they have a lane beside the road provided for walkers and bicyclists. And in the forests beautiful paths free from motorized vehicles make walking a pleasurable activity.

Several years ago my wife and I, along with our daughter, were vacationing in Garmisch, Germany. One beautiful Sunday morning we packed a typical German lunch of a bottle of wine, some cheese, sausage, fruit, and a loaf of bread. We then took the gondola ski lift to the top of the nearby mountain. As alpine mountains go, this was not especially high. We discovered that what we were doing was a very common thing for the Germans. At the top of the mountain were park benches placed here and there to capture the various scenic views. After a couple of hours absorbing the beauty of the area and watching a glider soaring overhead, we decided to descend. We had learned that there were beautiful trails down the mountain and so we had planned to make the return trip on foot. We expected that it would take most of the afternoon.

Anyone who has read *Heidi* will better understand our experience. The mountains were very much like those described in that delightful story. Hundreds of Germans strolled along on the well-designed and maintained footpaths. There was more than one way down and trails criss-crossed every so often, with signs at the junctions giving directions and the distances of alternative routes. To our surprise we noticed more people ascending the mountain than descending. I, more than either my wife or daughter, was to understand later in the day why this was so. It is better to walk up a mountain than down, as is also true of cross-country skiing. In descending, every step is a jar and strain on your shin muscles. Long before we reached the bottom I had misgivings about my completing the walk. But we finally made it to a little refreshment chalet where I welcomed the chance to rest and enjoy a cool drink. The remaining journey down was on a primitive road where I at least had the reassurance that if necessary I could hitch a ride the rest of the way.

I do not mean to color this delightful adventure with the one infirmity that only I experienced. The fact is that the walk down was so beautiful, the occasional vista so spectacular, and the experience so unique, that I would not hesitate a minute to do it again. Next time, however, I shall walk *up* the mountain, rather than *down*, and prepare physically in advance for the exertion. The slopes are quite gentle and anyone in normal physical condition can do it. It is a beautiful experience!

Although my wife and I have had many opportunities through the years to enjoy travel, sports, and recreation, as this book purports to reveal, there still are many things I would like to do. Among them are the various walking tours of Europe and the United States. There are many books published describing such tours for would-be walkers. Several are listed at the end of this chapter. They are fascinating reading, even if one doesn't actually take the tours. For example, there are books on walking through England, through Ireland, through Europe from north to south, through 100 cities of Europe, through English university and cathedral towns, and many more. They contain maps of the countryside and cities, information on shops, museums, hotels, and restaurants, historical background of the areas one walks through, and lists of the equipment needed.

For the United States, the Sierra Club has published a number of "Totebooks" which cover walking tours in national parks, California, the Smokies, other mountains, Yosemite Valley, and some beautiful

Taking photographs during walks is a most enjoyable hobby.

cities such as San Francisco. Their series also includes the Austrian and Swiss Alps, and several guides to backpacking, hut hopping, food for knapsacks, rock hounding, nature photography, and cooking on the trail.

If these books do not inspire you to adventurous walking, then by all means begin by sauntering around your neighborhood. You will be surprised at the many things you have missed in driving through this familiar area. Chances are you will see a friend with whom you will stop and chat, or get a new idea for your yard, or see and listen to a bird that serenades you as you pass. You will be enchanted at seeing your home territory in a new light.

Sauntering, it should be said, however, is not going to provide the ultimate pleasure of walking. To be healthful, and thus also enjoyable, walking should be done at a natural rhythmic pace that is different for each person. Stepping up your pace and lengthening your stride, or experimenting with them, ultimately should bring you to the most comfortable gait for you—one that will most benefit your physical condition and at the same time be the least tiring. Having achieved that, you may find yourself enthralled by the simple joys of walking, and like millions of others, you could become addicted.

There is a fine line between walking and hiking. I have discussed this difference in the chapter on hiking. It is largely the length of the walk, and whether camping and exploring are part of the outing. Walking is a pleasurable jaunt within a period of a day, while hiking implies an adventure of usually several days or more, and signifies "roughing it" in the woods or other unpopulated areas. Hiking usually requires backpacks and sturdy footwear. To be sure, the same trail may be used by both walkers and hikers, but usually only a segment of it is traversed by walkers.

Some of the most pleasant walks I have taken have been around the many lakes we have within the city where I live. While I am dismayed that Americans in general provide so little in the way of facilities for bicyclers, walkers, hikers, and the many participative sports, occasionally one finds an enlightened community that has developed areas such as lake fronts, riverside parks, and municipal playing fields. We are fortunate to live in such a progressive city, and a walk around one of our city lakes is a delightful experience. Along the stretches of woods, open grassy areas, and beaches the walk offers a constant change of activity—picnicking on the grass, archery, kite flying, napping, beach ball and swimming, sailing and fishing, bird watching, playground activity, softball, romance, sunbathing, bicycling, kayaking, various waterfront activities, a band concert, and horseplay among cavorting adults and youngsters. Such walks are above all mild and enjoyable exercise that improves both one's physical and mental condition. All this without spending a cent! Best bargain in the world!

I occasionally ponder why it is that I find jogging rather uninteresting but at the same time thoroughly enjoy walking. For one thing, undoubtedly where I walk as opposed to where I run has much to do with my different attitudes towards the two activities. When I walk, I generally seek out the most interesting route, often trying a new street, a previously unexplored block, or a nearby lake. Since I walk in ordinary street clothes I can traverse a park, a shopping area, and a residential area, and draw no attention to myself. In walking, I don't work up a sweat so that I have to get home to take a shower right away. Thus, I can sandwich in my walk along with a drive to a park or lake and not feel constrained to be back at any given time. Therefore, while I advocate jogging, if it doesn't turn you on, try brisk walking as an alternative. It won't do for you what jogging will, but it certainly beats sitting in a soft chair watching TV.

TIPS FOR OLDER WALKERS. As we get older one of the increasingly essential requirements for comfort is good footwear. Too

often we give up on activities because they hurt our feet or our legs. It has been said that legs appear to be among the first things to give out as we age. If this is true, I'd wager that if it isn't from lack of exercise, it too often is caused by cheap, ill-fitting, or badly designed and constructed shoes. With the mounting attention being given to physical fitness and the increased market for appropriate sportswear, manufacturers today offer a wide variety of good sports shoes. While many of the well-known brands are quite expensive, it is wise for anyone contemplating active participation in a sport such as walking, hiking, backpacking, jogging, golf, hunting, tennis, and others that require leg activity, to buy good-quality footwear designed for that sport. It will reduce sore muscles, back problems, and the concomitant frustration and discouragement which too often is blamed on "old age" rather than bad shoes.

Bill Merrill in his book, *The Hiker's and Backpacker's Handbook*, tells of hikers he has met on paths high in the California Sierras who were in their 70's and 80's. This gives testimony to the fact that the ability, or lack of it, to walk and hike is not always a function of age. It is, in fact, a favorite form of exercise among Americans over 60 who participate in any systematic program of physical activity.

A professor friend of mine for years daily walked the more than 2 miles from his office to his home. He was in his 60's and I assumed this regimen practically assured him of good health. It was to my surprise one day I learned he had suffered a heart attack. My immediate first reaction was to question whether such exercise did indeed help guard against these attacks, so I checked with my medical friends. I was told that had he not been exercising, his attack probably would have been fatal. As it is, he apparently fully recovered and now, some 15 years later, is happily retired and still walking around his neighborhood every day. Walking apparently saved his life.

As we get older we must recognize that we do not have the bounce we once had. Our spinal column doesn't cushion the jump or hop as it once did, and an accidental step on an irregular sidewalk or off a curb can be a jarring experience. It behooves us to keep a little closer watch on where we are going and what our footing is like. Recently while we were on an outing to the East Sea, between West Germany and Denmark, I was walking along with a fellow tourist when all of a sudden I found her sprawled on the sidewalk, handbag and umbrella flying. Fortunately, aside from torn hose, a bloody knee, and hurt pride, she was none the worse from the fall. Chatting as we had been, she simply had not paid attention to the footing below. In this northern climate the winters had gradually pushed some of the sidewalk blocks up and she had stumbled over one of them.

One of the adjustments I have made as I get older and walk outdoors in the wintertime is to wear crepe-soled shoes. This has several important advantages. First of all, such soles provide needed insulation against the cold ground or sidewalk, and thus add immeasurably to my comfort while walking. But equally important is the safety crepe soles provide when one unexpectedly steps on a patch of ice. A colleague of mine wears leather soles and heels throughout the year. I fear for his safety each time we walk across campus in winter, for he slips and slides and unnecessarily takes chances, it seems to me, on having *another* accident similar to one he had a couple of years ago.

For some, wearing bifocal glasses while walking can be a hazard. The reading correction in such glasses prevents one from seeing the walking surface clearly without unduly lowering one's head. If walking becomes for you a daily routine, you might want to check with your optician as to the best glasses to give sharp focus to the ground just in front of you. The newer type of multi-focus glasses may be helpful, especially those that have a continuous refraction adjustment rather than the sharp demarcation characteristic of bifocals. Or a separate pair of glasses for the purpose may be useful.

If walking has not been a regular part of your daily life, it should be recognized that a certain amount of stamina is required for vigorous walking of any distance. A gradual engagement in walking will improve one's endurance, and it is advisable, as in any physical activity, to extend the walk slightly each day rather than trying for long walks immediately from the beginning. I have noticed, for example, that a phenomenon occurs for me after about 1½ miles of rapid walking. Up to that time I feel no stress or fatigue, then almost suddenly there is a perceptible change. I feel a warmth and begin to shed my jacket or sweater. I have lost some of the bounce in my step and have to push myself a little to keep up the pace. Perhaps a dedicated distance walker doesn't experience such a feeling, but it reminds me of the marathon runners who apparently all go through a painful period about 2/3 into the run, and then, weathering that "wall," they are able to continue to the finish.

Building up endurance is especially important for aged participants. Recently my wife and I invited my 82-year old mother-in-law to go to Europe with us, an experience which she never contemplated having. Our concern was for her ability to negotiate the considerable amount of walking normally entailed in such a trip. We started her out on a gentle walk around the block. That in itself was an accomplishment for, in her small apartment, she had grown accustomed to shuffling from one room to another, losing her walking stride altogether. Within several weeks of daily walks she had regained her firm step and had no difficulty at all later in keeping up with us as we strolled the cobblestoned streets. Happily she has kept up her daily walks, once again having experienced the enjoyment and benefit of walking.

FOR MORE INFORMATION

The literature of walking is a joy unto itself, what with all the adventure it portrays and the dreams it inspires. So, reader, avail yourself of the reading if not the walking. Should you be moved to want to try walking on for size, you will want to have more information than I have given you. So hie yourself down to the nearest bookstore or your public library. Below are a few titles to start you off. Others will suggest more or perhaps different books for you to peruse. There are many good ones.

Calder, Jean. *Walking: A Guide to Beautiful Walks and Trails in America.* (Americans Discover America Series.) West Caldwell, N.J., Morrow, 1977. $3.95.

Fisher, Alan. *AMC Guide to Country Walks Near Boston Within Reach by Public Transportation.* Boston, AMC Books Div., 1977. $4.95.

Fletcher, Colin. *The New Complete Walker.* New York, Knopf, 1974. $10.00

Sierra Club, Totebooks Series. New York, Scribners.
> This series contains several of special interest to walkers. They are:
> *Hiker's Guide to the Smokies.* $7.95.
> *Hiking the Teton Backcountry.* $4.95.
> *Huts and Hikes in the Dolomites: A Guide to the Trails and Huts of the Italian Alps.* $4.95.
> *Hut Hopping the Austrian Alps.* $4.95.
> *Starr's Guide to the John Muir Trail and the High Sierra Region.* $4.95.
> *To Walk with a Quiet Mind: Hikes in the Woodlands, Parks and Beaches of the San Francisco Bay Area.* $5.95.

Sussman, Aaron, and Ruth Goode. *The Magic of Walking.* New York, Simon & Schuster, 1967. $7.50.

See also Chapter 17, "Hiking and Backpacking," for additional titles of interest to walkers.

4 *Birdwatching*

EVERYONE AT one time or another should try, from memory, drawing or painting a scene from nature. In sketching even such a prosaic thing as a barn, you may find to your astonishment that you really don't know what it looks like. I grew up on a farm and I thought I knew barns like the back of my hand. A few years ago I began to outline a typical barn, and for the life of me I couldn't remember how many hips the roof had. So I finished the sketch and then painted it as I remembered it to be. To this day I am still looking for a barn with two hips on each side!

Try drawing a tree. Surely anyone knows what a tree looks like. Drawing is not the art, observing is. We simply do not see the things around us. Recently, we have become interested in wildflowers and their identification. For all these years they were simply weeds, not the exquisite, dainty, beautifully designed flowers we now see. Photography also will sharpen one's observation powers. A ray of sunshine on a drop of water can be a beautiful thing when captured by a photographer's lens. Thumb through an issue of a photographic magazine and you will be amazed at the design, the color, the delicate forms of things familiar to you which you simply hadn't noticed before.

So it is with birds. Moreover, you can enjoy the double pleasure of both seeing *and* hearing them. Most of us take these beautiful creatures for granted. Seldom do we pause long enough to look and listen except, perhaps, when a blue heron laboriously wings its way across the lake, or a pileated woodpecker boldly lands on a tree trunk in front of you, or a loon calls out to its mate. Such instances may startle you, so you stop for an instant and give them your attention. But even then you may not really have seen them, as a birdwatcher might. They were dramatic enough for you to take note of for a moment, but you hasten along your way.

If there is one thing a birdwatcher needs it is patience. No one in a hurry can be a birdwatcher. Birdwatching forces you to slow down, stand still, wait, cock your ear, and keep out a sharp eye, as if you were expecting an apparition. The process itself is salutary. You are in the middle of a woods or park, along a stream or river, quietly observing some of nature's most spectacular creations. What better tonic for the harried soul?

Birdwatching as a hobby can mean different things to different people. For some, certainly beginners, it is cultivating the art of recognition or identification of different species. This ultimately can become a game, of course, compiling your checklist. Nothing wrong with that. But it inevitably will lead to other skills, for you must perforce learn about the habits and characteristics of various birds—where they feed and nest, when and if they migrate, their life cycle, their rarity, the differences between male and female, the pattern of their flights, their songs, and the variant species in different regions of the country. It can become an absorbing, lifetime hobby. It may improve your health and even your personality. I don't know a single dour, grouchy birdwatcher. In fact, given the choice, I would choose my friends from among birdwatchers. They are a fine lot!

Fortunately for those of us fairly new to birdwatching, there are several excellent field guides to bird identification. Also, beautifully illustrated bird books, with birds portrayed in detailed colored photographs, are available for closer study of your favorite species. But it probably will take more than field binoculars and a guidebook to get really started. It takes the help of experienced birding friends. With just such friends, during one long lunch period, I learned more about birds and wildflowers than I had from hours of poring over guidebooks to identify species I had seen. On the other hand, there are those who prefer solo field journeys. Simply being alone in the woods can provide auxiliary enjoyments. Also you may be challenged by the need to identify birds on your own, testing your acuity, and matching your perceptions to the field guidebook. Ultimately, as you develop your personal technique, and perhaps have identified the more commonly seen birds in your area, you may find it useful to join forces with others to seek out the less common species.

The biggest handicap a novice birdwatcher faces is discouragement. It is difficult to remember names outside the familiar circle of birds we have known since childhood. Sighting birds which are sitting still in a tree with enough light playing upon them is the exception rather than the rule. It is often too difficult to observe the various markings in sufficient detail to make a positive identification. Identifying birds by song, also, is not easy, since you have no easy field method of comparing the song you hear with a guide recording of bird songs. Some birds, however, do have distinctive flight patterns which aid in identification.

I have always envied my friends who are avid birdwatchers. They seem so absorbed in their hobby. It is easily apparent who is a dedicated birder and who is a novice. What interests me is the lengths to which serious birdwatchers will go to watch birds, or to catch a glimpse of a unique bird they know to be in a certain area. The depth of interest birdwatching develops strikes me as an important characteristic of this hobby which is especially suitable for retired people. It gives them a destination, and a purpose, for travel. And the areas they visit are generally beautifully wooded preserves pleasant to see even if one were not a birdwatcher. I have known birding to be the prime reason for some to travel great distances—to Russia, to island sanctuaries off the coast of Louisiana, to Canada, and through

Colorado. Of course, to be a birdwatcher one only has to open one's window, or step out in the backyard, or to install a bird feeder on a window ledge and watch the friendly birds appear.

One of the simple but delightful first steps one can take is to make or buy a hummingbird feeder, if you live in an area that has these precious little creatures. Recently, when we were camping in Colorado, we encountered a fellow camper who had rigged up several aluminum pie pans on the side of a tree, and put sweetened water in them. We counted more than a dozen hummingbirds flitting around these feeders. They brazenly buzzed us while we were eating at our table, nearly touching us as they darted to and fro.

Last winter, late in February, I was shoveling the light snow that had fallen during the night. It was a beautiful, still cold, but sunshiny day. Suddenly the air was pierced with the melodious song of a cardinal. There he was, at the very top of a neighbor's tall elm tree. With his cry of "What cheer, what cheer" my mind immediately was redirected from the grizzly, bitter winter we had just been through, to the inexorable rebirth of life that comes with every spring. No more joyous harbinger could one hope for. What cheer!

It has been estimated that there are no less than 5 million birdwatchers in this country. The American Birding Association is a rapidly growing organization, publishing its own magazine and promoting birdwatching as a hobby. Whether one establishes the goal of sighting the nearly 700 separate species of birds in the United States, or aspires to tackling the some 9,000 bird species world-wide, is not as important as positively identifying the scarlet tanager in your backyard.

The National Audubon Society, through its magazine, *Audubon*, inspires, guides, and entreats you to enjoy birds. How one does it is a personal matter. Identifying them, listening to them, watching them —all these—but above all developing a keen awareness of them has to be the beginning. They are so much a part of our existence that we too often pay no attention to them or, worse, do not even recognize their presence. Recently I was recording a letter on a cassette unit while sitting on the deck at our lake cabin. It wasn't until I played back what I had recorded that I heard the many birds singing in the background. The environment had been enriched with their songs and I hadn't even noticed. I vowed not to ignore such precious gifts again.

Among the various hobbies, birdwatching is probably the least expensive. It costs nothing to take a walk in the woods or park and enjoy birds. It is the easiest hobby in the world to follow. Soon, however, you may be interested in building or buying a bird feeder for your backyard, and some bird seed. Eventually, your curiosity will lead you to buy a bird book and then a pair of binoculars. Now you are ready to tackle the identity of birds beyond the sparrow, robin, and bluejay that we all know. At this point, you should go for a walk, either alone or with a friend who has been a birdwatcher, for a little tutoring is very helpful. He or she can tell you the tricks of field identification, and point out a few new species to you. Recently, I did just that and I learned to identify birds I didn't know existed in my area but which, apparently, had been there all the time. I just hadn't seen them.

If birdwatching grabs you, as it very well might, then you may want to join a local birdwatcher's club where you will be able to share experiences and learn from others where the best birding spots are in your area. The National Audubon Society has chapters in most population centers, more than 350 in all, and chances are there is one near you. If there is a university in your vicinity, check with its extension department. Most educational institutions now have opportunities for older people to take courses at little or no tuition cost, and you may find a course available on birdwatching.

TIPS FOR OLDER BIRDWATCHERS. The most exciting time to watch birds is early spring just as the migration season begins. Other seasons also can be enjoyable, particularly fall, when ducks and geese are heading south and blackbirds are holding their annual round-up. But the spring is the season when the great migration northward will bring unique specimens into your area, if only for a day or two. The time to observe them best is early in the morning. If you plan to go to the woods or a nearby swamp or lake, then you must dress more warmly than you might think is necessary from stepping outside your house to test the temperature. Watching birds requires that you stand still, sometimes for a long period, and the damp morning air will penetrate light clothing. Inevitably, you will become quite chilled after a little while. A down-filled ski jacket is excellent because it is lightweight and warm. If it has an attached hood, all the better; otherwise wear a warm headgear. Gloves, while comfortable, are awkward if you are using binoculars, which of course all birdwatchers do. But take some along to warm up your hands occasionally.

Birdwatching generally requires considerable walking. Therefore sturdy, comfortable shoes or boots are advisable. Since grass and weeds are wet in the early morning, footwear also should withstand moisture. Sporting goods stores have lightweight, rubberized boots that are ideal. Otherwise wear overshoes as you would on a wet day.

The walking involved in birdwatching is often over rough terrain, up and down hills, so one should be prepared for such exertion. Because of the many stops and starts, one does not tire from the pace,

A park naturalist explains the key to the birds to a happy student.

but it is not unrealistic to expect to walk a couple of miles, usually on footpaths, following bird sounds. Also, unless you are in familiar territory or on well-marked trails, it is possible to get lost, especially if you are alone. In such cases, a compass can be an aid in maintaining your orientation. You can easily become so absorbed in watching and listening for birds that your whereabouts may be overlooked. Keep alert for landmarks to help in finding your way out of the woods again.

Early spring also is an excellent time to observe certain woodland wildflowers. These bloom in the warm days before the leaves are out and while the sun can penetrate the woods. In fact, one is torn between looking down for wildflowers and looking up for birds. One can do both, of course, and most birdwatchers probably do. A little advance knowledge of early spring wildflowers can add to the enjoyment of the outing. There are excellent wildflower guidebooks available which aid in the identification of these delicate, dainty, and beautiful plants.

If you are handy with woodworking, you might want to build bird houses that will attract birds to your back yard or to nearby woods. Learning the feeding habits of various species and then providing feeders for them can bring the birds to you rather than your going out to the birds. This can be especially appealing to older folk who may not have the desire or ability to walk in the woods. The book by Walter E. Schutz, listed at the end of the chapter, has excellent illustrations of bird houses and bird feeders that are fairly simple to build. Housing and feeding birds, of course, is an attractive hobby for anyone, not just for older people.

An interest in birds can and probably will develop into other interests, particularly relating to conservation, ecology, the environment, and wildlife preservation. The maintenance of our wetlands, for example, is an essential factor in the migration and protection of our water birds. If ever you have an opportunity to drive through central Nebraska in March and early April you will be amazed to observe the great flocks of ducks, sand hill cranes, and Canadian geese. These majestic birds migrate through this area and are supported by the thoughtful provision of ponds, swamps, rivers, and lakes, some of which are beside and visible from Interstate 80. They are a memorable sight.

Of all the activities discussed in this book, none bridges the intergenerational gap better than birdwatching. Recently I observed the makeup of several organized groups visiting a bird sanctuary. The age of the participants ranged from very young children to quite elderly people walking with the aid of canes. There was no perceptible difference among them in their interest in the extraordinary display of water birds we were privileged to see that early morning. An interest in birds can be a life-long activity that is not dependent on physical capacity. In order not to miss the considerable pleasure that goes with the study of birds, youngsters *of all ages* should get started immediately.

If one lives within reasonable distance of a natural history museum, one can take advantage of its displays and exhibits of birds. Some museums place birds in life-like environments, so that one can study at close quarters the appearance and characteristics of birds that would be relatively difficult to view in the field. Such museums generally can be found on university campuses and are open to the public. Some public museums in large cities also are excellent, as are some zoological gardens.

FOR MORE INFORMATION

Because birdwatching is such a growing hobby there are many good books available to help the beginner or the experienced birder. Basic is a field guide, and eventually you will want to get one for your personal use. But your local public library can provide an array of books for you to test your interest. Some of those available are beautiful to look at and make good bedside reading. Following is a sample of the variety of publications available.

Books:

Bull, John, and John Farrand. *The Audubon Society Field Guide to North American Birds: Eastern Region.* New York, Knopf, 1977. $7.95.

Harrison, G. H. *Roger Tory Peterson's Dozen Birding Hot Spots.* New York, Simon & Schuster, 1976. $9.95.

Hickey, Joseph G. *A Guide to Birdwatching,* Rev. Ed. New York, Dover, 1975. $3.00.
A popularized text on the study of birds. The author was a scientist. Republished from an earlier book, but still useful.

Laycock, George. *The Bird Watcher's Bible.* New York, Doubleday, 1976. $2.95.
Covers a variety of subjects such as bird houses, birding vacations, blinds, and bird banding, and contains an identification list.

Line, Les, ed. *The Pleasure of Birds: An Audubon Treasury.* Philadelphia, Lippincott, 1975. $14.95.
The author, editor of *Audubon,* selected 25 articles from issues of that magazine which relate the characteristics of various birds. Written by naturalists who have made special studies of these birds and describe the pleasures of watching them. Contains beautiful photographs and illustrations. Interesting reading!

Mackenzie, John P. S. *The Complete Outdoorsman's Guide to Birds of Eastern North America.* New York, Pagurian Press, 1977. $9.95.

Pasquier, Roger F. *Watching Birds: An Introduction to Ornithology.* Boston, Houghton Mifflin, 1977. $9.95.

Peterson, Roger Tory. *A Field Guide to the Birds.* Boston, Houghton Mifflin, 1968, $4.95.
Similar in quality and content to Robbins, below.

Robbins, Chandler S., and others. *Birds of North America: A Guide to Field Identification.* New York, Golden Press, 1966. $4.95.
An authoritative, excellent handbook, filled with colored illustrations of birds, charts depicting songs, habitat location maps, flight patterns, and size information.

Schutz, Walter E. *How to Attract, House and Feed Birds.* New York, MacMillan, 1974. $3.95.

Udvardy, M. D. F. *The Audubon Society Field Guide to North American Birds: Western Region.* New York, Knopf, 1977. $7.95.

Wetmore, Alexander, and others. *Song and Garden Birds of North America.* Washington, D.C., National Geographic, 1964. $11.95.
One of the beautiful bird books. Portrays 327 species in color and fully describes them. An album of 6 records, presenting songs of 70 species, is in the back of the book.

Magazines:

Audubon. Bi-monthly. National Audubon Society, 950 Third Ave., New York 10022. $13.00 per year.

Birding. Bi-monthly. American Birding Association, Box 4335, Austin, Tex. 79765. $10.00 per year.

In addition, many states and regions publish birding magazines, often emphasizing local birds and sometimes named after the state bird. Check with your public library for such titles.

Bird Song Recordings:

Peterson, Roger Tory. "Field Guide to Western Bird Songs." Boston, Houghton Mifflin, 1972. Set of 3 records, $19.95; set of 3 cassettes, $23.95.

———. "Field Guide to Bird Songs." Boston, Houghton Mifflin. Set of 2 records, $17.95; set of 2 cassettes, $19.95.

Also see Wetmore, above.

5 *Frisbee® Disc*

MANY MIGHT assume that Frisbee® disc is a game only for young people. My wife and I thoroughly enjoy the sport, but since we are only in our early 60's we can't rightly speak for old people. We do know that it is a game that is appropriate for us.

The sport is blind to age differences. There is a talent and strategy involved that is equally applicable regardless of age. Recently, as we were camping with our adult children and their spouses in the mountains of central Colorado, we played, and my wife and I were just as expert as they. In fact, we appeared to be more consistent in our throwing.

It is a game that is especially good to combine with camping. In the evenings it affords a moderate amount of exercise after supper. No special area is required except a little open space. It is not restricted in the number of people who can play. And, not the least, the Frisbee disc takes no room in what is usually an overcrowded car on a camping outing.

In addition to the trademarked flying saucer manufactured and sold by Wham-O, there are many other brands on the market. The game, according to Dr. Johnson's book on the subject, is some 3 decades old. It consists of throwing a saucer-like plastic disc, about 1 foot in diameter, from one person to another. The deeply curved edges of the disc catch the air and cause it to float and veer off, depending on how it is thrown. There is a definite technique involved. Participants take pride in their ability to throw the Frisbee disc in such a way that it will float down exactly to the receiver. The receivers demonstrate their talents by catching the disc mid-air.

Because of the aerodynamics involved, the disc will react consistently given consistent conditions of air currents and launching. The challenge is in recognizing the exact angles to throw the disc so that it will respond correctly and as anticipated, taking account of the varying air currents.

Interestingly, this disc game has become a competitive sport in colleges. There are intercollegiate tournaments and international contests. It is even taught as a sport on some campuses.

Disc Golf is a new development which uses the disc instead of a golf ball to run a course. Players throw the Frisbee disc in an attempt to get it to land in the proximity of a basket on a pole. From there an easy toss, equivalent to a putt, puts the disc in the basket. Disc Golf courses are available in some resort campgrounds and are fun for participants of all ages.

The International Frisbee disc Association, with over 75,000 members around the world, with affiliate groups in England, Germany, Australia, Japan, Canada, Sweden, and other countries, promotes the enjoyment and competitive development of the game. A lifetime membership costing $3.00 includes a proficiency manual that should be useful in learning the elements of throwing and catching the flying disc.

The cost of the rotating disc, which goes under various trade names, is low, about the price of a modest lunch. In fact, it might not be a bad idea to spend your money for the disc rather than the lunch. The exercise and fun derived from playing with it is an appropriate alternative to overindulgence, of which many of us are guilty.

TIPS FOR OLDER FLYING DISC PLAYERS. The physical demands on a player are minimal. On the other hand, it is easy to become so involved, particularly in the catching of the flying disc, that one can overextend oneself. Older participants might be better able to control the throw if they were to study some of the techniques described in a manual.

Lest one believes that the sport is too frivolous or elementary to bother developing the techniques for throwing and catching the disc, one only has to watch some of the practitioners, say in a park or on

campus. It is surprising to see the precision and imagination exhibited by some of the more experienced players. One appreciates the skill even more after having tried to throw the Frisbee disc oneself. The disc literally performs for some of the more skillful players. It is convincing evidence that a Frisbee disc is more than a toy, and indeed there may be some rationale for intervarsity competition in this sport.

The flying disc is something that should become a regular item in your automobile, especially if you travel on extended trips. Unless you are different from others over 50, your legs begin to cramp after a few hours of driving. There is nothing better to relieve the muscles than to pull into a wayside or city park along the road and play for 15 minutes. It is fun and removes the boredom of travel. Not only does it exercise the legs, it is a good game to recondition the entire body. Follow the game with 10 minutes of jogging and you will be totally refreshed and ready to travel again.

FOR MORE INFORMATION

There is not a wide literature on Frisbee disc. Johnson's book is undoubtedly the most comprehensive. There have been technical studies of the aerodynamics of the rotating disc. For contests and competition there are rules. But one doesn't need a manual to enjoy the game. Just buy a Frisbee disc and start playing. Take it to the beach, or use your lawn or nearby park. Not only will you find it fun, you will soon discover a phenomenon observed by all players, that the disc has an almost magnetic attraction to tree trunks, passing pedestrians, and areas beneath parked cars.

Books:
Johnson, Stancil E. D. *Frisbee: A Practitioner's Manual and Definitive Treatise.* New York, Workman, 1975. $4.95.
This book, written by a psychiatrist and avid Frisbee disc player, tells you just about everything you would ever want to know about the sport. Profusely illustrated, it is interesting reading written with tongue-in-cheek. It has an amazing amount of detail and history of the sport.
Tips, Charles. *Frisbee for the Masters.* San Francisco, Celestial Arts, 1977. $4.95.
Written more from the standpoint of a competitive sport. Includes techniques of throwing and catching, aerodynamics, disc control, and training exercises.

6   *Camping*

MAN HAS AN indigenous yearning to return to his natural habitat. He constantly either seeks or attempts to develop a natural environment that includes trees, brooks, birds, lakes, and other aspects of nature. Our present mode of living, however, effectively thwarts our efforts, and increasingly we surround ourselves with bricks and mortar. To those who are fortunate enough to have friends or relatives who live on farms, a visit now and then to a rural area is a refreshing change from urban living. Canoe trips offer one of the best of the few remaining opportunities to live in the woods. Camping in wilderness areas, if one can choose one's sites carefully, can also allow one to experience the joy and peace only to be found in a retreat from our urbanized society. In the wilderness one can find the tranquility of nature, where cooking over the open campfire adds a special flavor to the food, putting zest in the appetite and peace in the soul.

Regrettably even most camping today fails to provide the benefits of a true camping experience. Certainly it provides no solitude. Cross-country camping has lost most of its appeal because of the crowded campsites and the prevalence of motorized camping equipment. Mountain camping, backpacking, river rafting, and canoe trips still hold to the basics of wilderness living, however. And occasionally, one can still find public campgrounds in some remote areas that offer the old-fashioned camping experience.

Recently, my wife and I visited what, laughingly, was called a "camping show." If we expected to see an array of the latest in camping equipment, we were in for disappointment. What we saw on display instead was the great variety of *motorized motels* that the industry has developed. We were not completely surprised, because on our cross-country camping trip the previous summer we had been among the few families still using tents. Campgrounds were filled with a fascinating variety of equipment ranging from pup tents (us), to motorcycle-drawn trailers, to unbelievably large motor homes that had considerable difficulty maneuvering into campsites.

Aside from canoe camping trips (described in the chapter on canoeing), our many memories include the camping trips we took as a family over the years. One such was through Canada and New England. This took place some 15 years ago, when most camping was still done in tents and often with an open campfire. Because we camped at every opportunity then, I had converted a one-wheel trailer to a camping unit. The trailer body had a top that, when removed, served as our table. In the trailer we carried our tent, sleeping bags, air mattresses, camp stools, and other necessary camping equipment. The trailer had a tailgate that opened to form a cooking counter. The rear of the trailer had a cabinet which held our cooking gear and utensils easily available to form the kitchen. This rig made camping easy and pleasurable, even in inclement weather, for we were adequately prepared with a tarpaulin, camp stove, and rain gear.

One particular event still stands out as one of the highlights of that trip. We were camping in Acadia National Park in Maine. A lobster fisherman who lived near the campground had a sign by the road announcing that he sold freshly caught and cooked lobsters. Toward evening we visited him and bought one for each of us. We took these steaming delicacies back to the campground for the most elegant camp meal we had ever experienced.

Perhaps the most beautiful camping site we ever had was at Grand Teton National Park in Wyoming. The campground was on the edge of Jenny Lake. Across the lake rose, as if from the water itself, the majestic Teton Range. As Freeman Tilden stated, in his book on the national parks, "The impression made on the memory by the Teton Range, once seen, is indelible." Except for the fact that a bear ravaged part of our food supply one night, it was a perfect camping experience.

Our introduction to camping was inauspicious, however. We were totally inexperienced, obviously, and almost totally unequipped. We had heard about the joys of camping, so we decided to give it a try. We chose for our debut the Rocky Mountain National Park. Our equipment consisted of 2 army cots, 2 blankets, some cooking utensils for an open campfire, but no tent or tarpaulin. All went beautifully, with a nice campfire in the evening under the stars. We sang our usual family songs, and then finally bedded down, with the 2 children sleeping in the car and my wife and I on the cots. Being plains folk we didn't know the ways of mountain weather. Sometime in the night we felt the first drops of rain. We scrambled around, found an old chenille bedspread in the car, and with it made a lean-to to protect us from the rain. Luckily it never rained hard, but it did sprinkle heavily off and on the rest of the night. We also hadn't prepared for the cold night air common in the mountains. We kept adding clothes, until by morning I had on not only my pajamas but also 2 pairs of overalls, my shirt and jacket, and a towel wrapped around my head. As soon as daybreak arrived I started a campfire and brewed some coffee. We both were so stiff we could hardly move.

Soon after that rather hectic experience, either despite or because of it, we invested in a tent, tarpaulin, warm sleeping bags, air mattresses, and other equipment for cooking. We had learned that army cots not only are superfluous but are in fact very cold to sleep on because the cold air hits you from underneath. It is better to sleep on the floor of the tent with an air mattress or on a piece of foam rubber.

Camping has taken a major turn since those earlier days. No

longer are you dependent on national, state, and municipal parks for campsites. Located along all major highways are privately run, well-organized campgrounds. These have showers, laundry facilities, groceries, and even occasionally movies and swimming pools. Also, since these campgrounds are designed mostly for the motor campers, hookup facilities for electricity and water are available at each campsite. As a bow to the few remaining tent campers, like ourselves, there may be some sites for tenters, with a picnic table and perhaps a fire pit at each site. Charges for rental of the site and the use of showers and other facilities may be $4.00 or more per night.

Tent camping today still can be fun. It is less fun than it used to be on cross-country trips staying in organized campgrounds because of the tenters' social status (or lack of it). This is especially noticeable when you camp in rainy weather. Misery loves company, they say, and when you are enduring the adversities of the weather while others in the campground are sitting in their comfortable motel on wheels, watching television, and feeling pity (or disdain) for you, you even begin to feel sorry for yourselves. Perhaps it is just as well, under those circumstances, to get a motel room until conditions improve. That is one of the few concessions I am willing to make to my getting older. During younger days I used to enjoy the adversity as a sort of defiance of our affluent society.

Having seemingly disparaged the motor home as a form of camping, let me quickly say that for many people it provides a viable alternative to the high costs of motels and restaurants. This is especially true for families with several children. It also is one answer for retired people who travel for several months out of a year. They can carry with them personal belongings for their pleasure or comfort; it gives them access to some beautiful outdoor areas where motels may not be available; and they needn't worry as much about where they are going to spend the night. Also, they have their own familiar bed every night. Since the distances traveled daily are not likely to be long, the size of this vehicle is not a severe burden.

WHERE TO GO CAMPING.   One only has to observe highway traffic in the summer to be convinced that the American public has taken to the roads in campers of every description. One in 5 American families goes camping. The National Recreation and Park Association estimates that camping has grown 500 percent in the last 10 years. The camping vehicle industry is one still growing today, despite threatened gasoline shortages, with some 3 million recreational vehicles on the roads. To accommodate the expanding demand for campsites, there are some 20,000 public and private campgrounds across the United States. In addition there are national parks and over 150 national forests with camping facilities. Campers use published directories, such as the ones listed at the end of this chapter, to plan their stops as they travel cross-country. Highway maps, particularly the official state highway maps, generally indicate with symbols the various campsites within each state. They are helpful in the preliminary planning of one's trip.

CAMPING EQUIPMENT. There are several basic types of recreational camping vehicles, varying in cost and design from modest to luxurious. Truck campers are one of the most popular. They are basically a living unit placed on the bed of a pickup truck. These can be removed when the family is not camping and the truck can be used for other purposes. It is this versatility that accounts in part for the truck's popularity, in addition to the fact that it doesn't require towing a trailer.

Travel trailers are perhaps the most popular mobile home. They come in varying lengths from the fairly compact to the over 30-foot long luxurious home on wheels. They are easily towed and, when they are parked, the car or vehicle towing the trailer can be detached and used for local transportation. Travel trailers are ingeniously designed, comfortable, and well equipped.

Motor homes are self-powered camping vehicles. They range in size from 18 feet to well over 30 feet. The longer models boggle the mind when they enter the campgrounds. They do indeed look like motorized motels and, not having experienced using them, I do not fully understand the necessity for the large size. The smaller motor homes are very comfortable and usually have beautifully designed interiors, including fully equipped bathrooms. One problem in their use, as with the truck camper, is that there is no transportation available once you have parked for camping. For that reason one occasionally sees such vehicles towing a small compact car or carrying a motorcycle.

Although motorized camping seems to be dominating cross-country travel, there still are many uses for tents. Canoeing, backpacking, mountaineering, fishing the backwaters, and visiting remote park areas, such as Isle Royal National Park in Lake Superior, which do not permit motorized vehicles—all require tents for camping. Although the opportunities for ingenuity are somewhat limited, each year one finds new designs in tents. Tents range in size from the very lightweight nylon pup tent suitable for 1 or 2 people, to large family-sized compartmentalized tents with porch-like awnings. Pup tents are especially useful when one has to carry the camping gear, as on canoe or hiking trips. The large tents are desirable if you have a large family, when the gear can be hauled in the car or trailer, and when you set up camp and stay generally in one site.

If the camping experience is to be successful, one needs to have certain basic equipment and supplies. A good camping book will provide a checklist to follow. Successful camping is more than just an inexpensive way of eating and sleeping. The most pleasure comes from the activities usually associated with camping—enjoyment of the woods, hiking, observing nature, exploring, birdwatching, rock collecting, beachcombing, star-gazing, fishing, mountain climbing, canoeing, and socializing. Campers generally are a friendly lot, and trading experiences and making acquaintances are part of the fun.

THE COST OF CAMPING.   This will vary greatly depending on many factors. While it is probably true that many families camp because they "want to get away from the city and back to nature," some are likely to be motivated by the fact that camping reduces traveling costs. Such savings will not be realized during the first year or two while equipment costs are amortised. But good tents and sleeping bags, properly cared for, will last for many years. A couple can outfit themselves with high-quality camping gear for less than $1000, if they do tent camping. If they invest in wheeled equipment the costs will vary from upwards of $2000 for a camping trailer— literally a tent on wheels that folds down for travel—to more than $20,000 for some of the luxurious motor homes. Those that opt for the motor homes are obviously not motivated by cost savings, but rather by a desire to enjoy a mode of traveling that appeals to them. It is doubtful that the economics of motor home travel can alone justify the purchase of such equipment if it is only used for vacations.

Before investing in the purchase of a motor home, some advise renting one for a week or two. Not only will you determine whether or not it appeals to you, you will also be able to evaluate the features, size, and other characteristics of the equipment.

One of the most touted and well-organized travel trailer groups is the Wally Byam Club, promoted by Airstream, those silver bullet-like trailers seen literally all over the world. Owners have registered vehicles with plainly seen registration numbers. Directories of owners provide instant identification of the trailer you see on the highway or in campsites. There are organized rendezvous in various parts of the country, with planned activities in and around the campgrounds. These clubs, only one of many such organizations promoted by the manufacturers of travel trailers and other groups, are especially geared for retired people who have the time to participate in leisurely travel. I recall once viewing a fascinating Airstream movie about such a caravan on its travels through Africa. It portrayed the spirit and adventure of a safari, not without its occasional adversity.

Trailers are increasingly used as substitutes for summer homes. Many trailer parks, often located on lake shores, are designed for semi-permanent guests who may park their trailers and return to them on weekends or for vacation. In such a situation, one becomes part of a camping community, and familiar with one's neighbors.

It used to be that to go camping was tantamount to "roughing it." That is hardly true today, even with tent camping. A camper who is properly equipped can be comfortable, eat well, and enjoy the natural surroundings, away from the pressures of everyday life. Camping must be contagious, for there is an epidemic of the camping bug that has infested millions of people. If you haven't tried it, you ought to get exposed.

TIPS FOR OLDER CAMPERS. If, indeed, you haven't camped before and want to try it, prepare well for it. Some of our friends who did not follow this admonition found their camping outing to be disastrous and never tried it again. One is well advised to start out easy. Begin by borrowing or renting good equipment and take it on a weekend to a beautiful camping spot—a state-operated park, for example. Also pick a weekend during which good weather is expected. It is important to have a positive experience the first time out. It would be most advantageous if you could go camping with friends who are experienced campers. There are a number of tricks or techniques that add to the enjoyment of camping that can best be learned from such friends.

Campers, I suspect, are convinced that they are a hardy spartan group who enjoy the challenge of pitting themselves against the odds of surviving without all the modern conveniences we have come to believe are necessary. The fact is that few people really enjoy truly primitive living. One only has to observe the lengths to which campers go to fix up their campsites to be almost as comfortable and convenient as their homes. Therefore, face your camping experience realistically. Don't go camping with the idea that you want to prove something unless it is in your nature to take up such challenges. Better to plan to make yourself as comfortable as possible so that you can focus your attention on some of the great rewards of camping rather than worrying about being uncomfortable.

In the same vein, use your camping experience as an opportunity for an eating adventure. To cite an example, I will wager that bacon and eggs, or pancakes and sausage, or French toast and hot syrup, on your first morning out, will be one of the greatest eating pleasures of your life. I shall never forget the thrill, yes, literally the thrill, that our group had while on a canoe trip. We were 3 days paddling away from all civilization. My wife had brought along the makings for an apple pie. One day in the middle of the afternoon I started a good campfire next to a large rock. I set up our reflector oven and placed it in front of the hot coals. We then placed the pie in the oven and we all went fishing for a couple of hours. When we returned, the coals had died out and in the oven was one of the most beautiful apple pies any of us had ever seen. You can bet that was an eating adventure!

For older campers the admonition to prepare well so as to be comfortable applies especially to clothing. One of the surprises for new campers is that living in the woods exposes one to raw winds, chilly nights, and occasionally damp days. The opposite can also be true; that is, there can be days when the weather is very hot, and one must cope with enervating sun. Taking along appropriate clothing for these extremes in the weather can make the difference between success or failure for your outing. Weatherproof footwear is particularly important, as is rain gear. If one were to identify the main difference between young and old campers, it would be, in my opinion, the emphasis that the older camper places on comfort. And while it is vital that comfortable facilities—that is, tent, sleeping bag, and air mattress—are provided, I believe it is of equal if not more importance to have along appropriate clothing to assure personal comfort.

Lest older people fear that camping is a demanding activity suitable only for the hale and hearty, I think it should be pointed out that this is something anyone in reasonable health can do. It is not burdensome. It does not require strength. It is not physically difficult or exhausting. One does not need to have endurance. In short, it really is a mild activity that is especially well suited for older people. One of my memorable camping experiences took place less than 2 months after I had a slipped-disc operation. Obviously I was in no position to lift anything, so my family put up the tent and readied the camp. We camped for about 4 days at the Jenny Lake Campground in the Grand Teton National Park. We had comfortable air mattresses and sleeping bags, and I had no difficulty at all from the experience. As I recall the worst aspect was the long automobile ride to and from the park.

FOR MORE INFORMATION

Preparing for the camping trip is half the fun of camping. It is necessary to learn a great deal about a lot of things—tents, air mattresses, sleeping bags, the necessities to take along—cooking equipment, food, and so on. A good book can be invaluable to provide this background and also to remind one of the items one must bring along. Most good books will have equipment checklists, as well as directory information as to where to go camping or how to find such information. Your public library and bookstore will have such books.

Books:

Belt, Forest H. *Easi-Guide to Camping Comfort.* Indianapolis, Howard W. Sams & Co., 1974.

Recognizing that being uncomfortable has cooled many people's interest in camping, the author stresses how comfort can be achieved while camping. Also useful in selecting tents, what to look for in design and features.

Harland, Arline P., and Edgar N. Harland. *Traveling with Tent and Trailer.* Beverly Hills, Ca., Trail-R-Club of America, 1973. $3.95.

A highly personalized account, which gives the would-be trailer camper an insight into what is in store for him. Useful bibliography of publications on trailering.

Merrill, W. K. *All About Camping.* Harrisburg, Pa., Stackpole, 1970. $3.95.

Comprehensive guide, written by a park ranger. Somewhat dated (original copyright is 1962), but still very useful for the woods camper.

Rand McNally Campground & Trailer Park Guide. Skokie, Ill., Rand McNally, 1976. $6.95.

Lists and describes over 20,000 campgrounds in the U.S., Canada, and Mexico. There also are regional editions for western and eastern sections of the U.S.

Winchester, James H. *Camping Guide.* Clearwater, Fl., Snibble, 1973. $1.00.

A shirt-pocket sized guide that is very useful. Packs in a great deal of information in a small book.

Woodall's Campground Directory. 11th North American Edition. Published annually. Highland Park, Ill., Woodall, 1977. $6.95.

Lists over 18,000 inspected, approved, and rated campgrounds.

Magazines:

Camping Journal. 8 issues per year. Davis Publications, Inc., 229 Park Ave. South, New York 10003. $6.95 per year.

Motorhome Life. 9 issues per year. Trailer Life Pub. Co., 23945 Craftsman Rd., Calabasas, Ca. 91302. $7.50 per year.

Trailer & RV Travel. Monthly. Woodall Publishing Co., 500 Hyacinth Place, Highland Park, Ill. 60035. $7.50 per year.

Trailer Life. Monthly. Trailer Life Pub. Co., 23945 Craftsman Rd., Calabasas, Ca. 91302. $7.50 per year.

Covers camper, trailer, and motor home activities. Available also on newsstands.

Trails-A-Way. Twice monthly. TAW Publishing Co., 9731 Riverside Dr., Greenville, Mi. 48838. $3.00 per year.

Wilderness Camping. Bi-monthly. 1597 Union St., Schenectady, N.Y. 12309. $6.95 per year.

Regional or State Guides:

Little, Mildred. *Camper's Guide to Texas Parks, Lakes and Forests.* Houston, Tex. Gulf Publishing Co., 1977. $4.95.

An example of a good regional guide.

7 *Hunting*

WHO AMONG us has not thrilled at the honking of Canadian geese in the night as they wing their way southward in the fall? I am always reminded of Jack London's *Call of the Wild* as I cock an ear and follow the sound. I imagine them to be sending me a message, reminding me that winter is on the way, and preparations must be made. For sure, geese flying south are a harbinger of colder weather soon to come. While on the farm we always heeded these signs, more accurate than today's 10 o'clock weather forecast.

For many, autumn begins with the opening day of the hunting season. There is an excitement in the air as you and your friends plan for that day, oiling up your guns, selecting the ammunition, and plotting your destination. For some it will mean the smell and taste of delicious wild game on the table. For others they will go along "for the exercise," or "to get outdoors." Either way, hunting in the crisp autumn air, among the rustling leaves and stalks, is reward enough.

Pheasant hunting used to be an annual event in my life. It was a time for good friends to spend the day walking together in the woods and fields. It was the outing that was important. It was the season to be out-of-doors, to test our little-practiced skill of shooting at a fast-moving target. We knew the odds were in favor of the pheasants, but that merely increased our sense of challenge.

I recall one such day when I joined a group of friends who were far more professional than I. Anyone could see that. They had proper hunting togs, ammunition belts, newly oiled 12- and 16-gauge shotguns, and that air of know-how that quickly tells them which field to cover. I simply followed along, with my small 410-gauge, single-shot gun, my wool slacks, and oxfords—hardly proper attire to be wading through tall corn stalks. I wasn't especially alert either as the first flush of pheasants exploded from the cornfield in front of me. With an involuntary reflex action I raised my gun and shot. To everyone's surprise, and especially mine, down came a bird. Instantaneously, I became a respected member of the group, almost to my later regret. For the rest of the day, despite my increasing weariness, I had to join the group on every block and drive through the fields. You see, mine was the only pheasant shot that day. I was a proud and tired father when I came home to my family that night. But leave it to a child to call the shot as it really is. My small daughter exclaimed when she saw the one pheasant I brought in, "Daddy, is that all you got?" Little did she know how much that bird represented to me.

Why do people hunt? I'm not going to answer that question for anyone else but myself. I am sure there is a kinship among regular hunters, which I am not, that would invoke a common answer to that question. To me hunting is a romance, an adventurous enjoyment of nature. For others it may be the competition, the "sport" of bagging game that attracts them. To each his own. Let me join my brother on the old family farm in Nebraska on a beautiful bright morning after a soft snowfall. We will trek through the woods for a mile or 2, following the nearly dry creek bed that brings back a host of memories. He will loan me his .22 Winchester and he'll take his favorite 12-gauge. We'll call it hunting more as an excuse to go rather than as a mission to stock the dinner table. What are we hunting for? Well, now, let's see. After such a snowfall, the rabbits and squirrels will be sitting pretty tight. On the other hand, fresh snow will reveal rabbit tracks, telling us of their whereabouts. Our dog will sense any movement of squirrels. It should be a good morning for hunting, but just in case, I'll take my camera. There should be some beautiful scenes among the woods and streams, especially with the glistening sun. Perhaps that gives you my answer as to why I hunt.

Hunting, it has been said, is a bigger sport, and bigger business, in some areas, than football or any other. It, more than most activities, is a conglomerate sport that encompasses a wide range of experiences, from simple rabbit hunting in the nearby woods to a major safari in Africa. Each type of hunting requires its own equipment, guns, dogs, guides, expertise, and expense. As an indication of the variety of hunting activities one could list deer hunting with a bow and arrow; duck hunting with blinds, boats, and dogs; antelope hunting with pack horses and camp gear; big game hunting with trips half way round the world; coyote hunting with airplanes; and fox hunting with trained horses and hound dogs. One can hunt small game, upland game, big game. Some hunters hunt for trophies, others for food, some go for companionship, some to enjoy the out-of-doors, others for the challenge, and some to rid the area of varmints. What kind of hunting should you do? The modern answer is: Whatever turns you on.

There are hunters, of course, for whom hunting is their most absorbing hobby or sport. Few of us reach that point. But it doesn't require much in the way of guns, equipment, or expense to try your hand at hunting rabbits or squirrels or pheasant or grouse. If you like it you may want later to try duck hunting, or even go after antelope or deer. The bug will have bitten you if you find yourself dreaming of hunting wild boar or bear, elk or moose, and picturing that trophy on your den wall.

Let's simply get you started on small game. Beyond that you can advance to any stage you wish, but you'll have to get your information from the many books and magazines available on hunting. To start, you probably should buy or borrow one of two guns which I found to be the minimum—a .22 caliber rifle or a 12-gauge shotgun.

Your sporting goods store can advise you on this. I also had a beautiful single-shot 16-gauge that I gave to my daughter-in-law. It is an ideal beginning gun for a woman—lightweight, adequate, and fun. Some may argue that a beginner needs a repeater, since he or she may not be able to hit the target with one shot. However, a beginner generally also lacks the skill to get off the second round accurately on a fast-moving target, so the outcome with a single or a multiple shot will be about the same, except for the amount of ammunition used.

Once you have your gun or guns, you had better do some target practicing. Where to do this may be somewhat of a problem. The principle is the same as going to a golf driving range to practice before you play golf. Once in the field you should be hunting, not practice shooting. Throughout the country there are rod and gun clubs, sometimes called sportsmen's clubs. These generally provide their members the opportunity to practice shooting clay pigeons or skeet. Hunters use trap shooting and skeet shooting both as sports in themselves and as pre-hunting season refreshers.

There is, of course, the matter of the license. Hunting anything requires a license. And the costs of these are going up annually. One of my annoyances with hunting and fishing licenses is that the various states fail to cooperate in honoring other states' licenses. If you are retired and are traveling about the country, doing a little hunting and fishing as you go, you've got to get not only a license in each state, but a nonresident license at sometimes exorbitant cost whenever you are out of your home state. This is one area in which I hope senior power will bear results. Perhaps a national license, or a senior citizen license good in all states, will be a reality some day. It would be a great boon for would-be senior sportsmen.

So you have your gun, your license, and you have been practicing on the shooting range. All this should be done before autumn, for the seasons start early, generally in September for grouse. This is followed by waterfowl and pheasant seasons, with rabbit and squirrel hunting opening at the same time, probably with open season throughout winter. When you get your license you will be given a booklet that will outline the seasons for you.

Where to go hunting may seem like a difficult problem, and in some ways it is. Increasingly, it seems, farmers have posted no hunting signs in their fields, preventing pheasant and rabbit hunters from getting to their chosen hunting spots. This has occurred not because the farmers are becoming cantankerous (they generally are, in fact, very generous) but because some hunters are careless or thoughtless, sometimes tearing down fences, leaving gates open, or even accidentally shooting a cow or other farm animal. You no doubt can get information on where to hunt from state conservation and recreation offices, state fish and game departments, sporting goods stores, or hunting friends in the area. All should be helpful in providing leads as to good hunting spots. There are books published (such as the Knap book listed below) that also provide a state-by-state guide to fishing and hunting. But good hunting places are giving way to highways, industrial growth, airports, and big farming which drains lowlands and swamps.

Hunters also are likely to get caught up in other activities. For example, duck hunters often are greatly concerned about conservation, particularly the draining of wetlands. Such organizations as Ducks Unlimited lobby for the preservation of feeding and breeding places for waterfowl. The future of hunting for ducks, geese, and other migratory game birds may well be limited if most of our wetlands disappear.

Hunting is not necessarily always done with a gun. Some of the finest hunting, and for many, the most enjoyable, is hunting with the camera. All the preparation of hunting trips, the enjoyment of the outdoors, and stalking of the prey is shared by both the hunter with the gun and the hunter with the camera. Both shoot, one to kill, the other to capture in a photograph. The cameraman, on the other hand, is not limited in his hunting to animals or live game. He can focus on the many beauties of nature as he moves through the woods, mountains, or freshly fallen snow. Camera hunting provides one the opportunity to combine hobbies, and doesn't require a license!

Another adjunct interest that may develop from hunting is the breeding and training of hunting dogs. A hunter and his dog are like brothers, or perhaps father and son is a better analogy. The dog must be intelligent, disciplined, and interested. A well-trained pheasant dog can mean the difference between being blanked and getting your bag limit. Each type of hunting requires a special breed of dog, and whether you raise and train a dog for your own use, or as a hobby, you will need to know a great deal both about hunting and about dogs.

Trophy hunting can be an exotic and expensive hobby, a totally different kind of experience than, let's say, pheasant hunting. A couple of years ago my wife and I had heard of a trophy collection at a small bar in Paxton, in central Nebraska. So on our way to Colorado on our annual skiing trip we stopped to see what it was about. We weren't quite prepared for what we saw. It was a one-man natural history museum of extraordinary scope, personally collected by the owner of the bar. Annually for years he took safaris, covering all parts of the globe, adding to his collection. It was well worth the stop to see his large display and visit with this unusual hunter.

Not every season, but if one is lucky . . .

Some hunters, and I suppose occasionally nonhunters, develop an interest in gun collecting. It probably begins by gradually accumulating a rack of guns with which you hunt, since different types of hunting require different guns. Ultimately, however, collecting guns can become an objective in itself. If ever you are bitten by the collecting bug, whether it is guns, stamps, antique cars, rare books, rocks, or old coins, be prepared to dedicate a considerable amount of your time, and probably money, to this activity. There is a contagion about collecting not fully understood but it can be an enjoyable, absorbing hobby.

TIPS FOR OLDER HUNTERS. Many types of hunting are fairly demanding, physically. Generally it is a sport that tends to favor the person willing to cope with the elements. Usually it requires considerable walking, often through woods, brush, fields, along streams, and in weather that may at times be on the unpleasant side. In short, it is not a sport for the faint-hearted. Certainly before one embarks on a hunting outing, whether for deer, pheasant, coyotes, rabbits, grouse, or ducks, it would be well to be assured that the stress of the outing is not beyond one's physical capacity. Each opening day of hunting season will offer news accounts of hunters who have gone beyond their endurance and have suffered the consequences. Too often people have not prepared for the physical strain of hunting by advance exercising and training. The sedentary office worker is usually ill-prepared for hunting.

Assuming you have the fitness to embark on a day's hunting or a longer outing, you can enjoy the many facets of hunting. For example, one seldom hunts alone. One is associated with people who have a common interest. Companionship is one of the real benefits of hunting. For that reason choosing one's companions is important. For instance, it doesn't seem very prudent to select a companion who is careless with guns. Nor does a drinking partner add much to the peace of mind one would like to have with a hunting companion, particularly because of the safety concern. Compatibility is important. The hunting party will probably experience some hardships, so all members should be able to gracefully accept them without grousing. People with a sense of humor can be a great asset. Who wants to be criticized just because he missed a bird? It is a lot more fun if you all can laugh about it.

Dress appropriately for the hunt. That doesn't mean you have to invest in a lot of fancy hunting togs. They won't aid you much in bagging game. Nevertheless, hunting attire is designed to withstand the wear and the weather, and offer the comfort that other clothes may not. It is important for us older folk to dress for comfort particularly. Your attitude toward hunting will not be very positive if you are chilled to the bone, or wet to the skin. You must remember that if your hunt requires rather strenuous walking, you will become warm. Then when you stand around and wait, as in a block and drive for pheasant, or in deer and antelope hunting, you will probably get cold. A combination of clothing that will assist you in adjusting to these varying conditions is advisable. Hunting is not unlike cross-country skiing in this respect—it is best to wear clothes that can be removed in layers as the need arises, and easily put on again, rather than wearing one heavy coat that provides all or nothing protection.

It is terribly easy, while hunting, to get lost in the woods. Especially on a cloudy day you can lose your orientation very quickly. One becomes so intent on the hunt that often the thought of where he is going or where he is at the moment doesn't occur to a hunter until it is too late. Then panic can set in, especially if darkness is approaching. The wise hunter will always carry a whistle or small horn so that he can let his companions know where he is. Have some pre-arranged plan of how to contact one another or sound a signal, such as an automobile horn, to provide guidance for the lost hunter. Modern electronic equipment greatly facilitates communication in the field. For example, two-way walkie-talkies are ideal, not only for orientation but also for effective communication of the presence of game, as in coyote hunting. If your car is equipped with a citizen's band radio, as many of them are today, the first one back to the car can contact the other hunters with walkie-talkies and guide them back. The only excuse one has for getting lost is carelessness, and the older one is, the more important it is not to add panic to an already strenuous day. A little planning can avoid it.

Carelessness and hunting do not mix. A hunter is walking around with a lethal weapon and must give it its due respect. The proper handling of a gun must be thoroughly understood before you ever load in the ammunition. One cardinal rule is never to point a gun, loaded or unloaded, in the direction of another person. If you are walking, keep your gun pointed down toward the ground. Be prepared for that occasional stumble so that should the gun discharge, no one will be directly in front of you. Keep the safety catch on until you are ready to shoot. Be especially careful while climbing over or through a fence so that the gun doesn't accidentally discharge, hitting you or a companion. Don't let your gun barrel hit the ground or snow. It could plug up and then burst when you fire. Don't climb a tree with a loaded gun. It could fall and discharge. If you are shooting, make certain there is no one in your line of fire beyond your view. That is especially important when shooting a rifle because of the distance its bullet will carry. Avoid shooting at surfaces where the bullet could glance off and hit an unsuspecting target.

Don't bring a loaded gun indoors or set it down where children could get at it. That probably is enough "don'ts" and "do's" to illustrate that hunting is not for casual, careless people.

FOR MORE INFORMATION

Hunting has so many ramifications that all I've tried to include is a sampling of what it may involve. Get yourself a couple of good hunting or sports magazines and thumb through them and you will soon find yourself dreaming of all sorts of field activities. Your bookstore, sporting goods dealer, and public library can supply books and magazines on any aspect of hunting that appeals to you. Following are a few titles that will indicate the variety of reading available. Even if you don't hunt, reading about it is enjoyable.

Books:

Cabell, Charles A., and David St. Clair. *Safari: Pan Am's Guide to Hunting with Gun and Camera Around the World.* New York, Doubleday, 1969. $5.95.

Cone, Arthur L., Jr. *Complete Guide to Hunting.* New York, Macmillan, 1970. $6.95.

Dickey, Charles. *Charles Dickey's Quail Hunting.* Birmingham, Al., Oxmoor House, 1974. $2.95.

Elliott, Charles. *Outdoor Observer: How to See, Hear and Interpret in the Natural World.* New York, Dutton, 1970. $4.50.

Elman, Robert, ed. *All About Deer Hunting in America.* New York, Scribners, 1976. $10.00.

Hill, Gene. *A Hunter's Fireside Book: Tales of Dogs, Ducks, Birds and Guns.* New York, Winchester Press, 1972. $7.95.

James, David, and Wilson Stephens, eds. *In Praise of Hunting.* Old Greenwich, Conn., Devin-Adair, 1961. $10.00.

Janes, E. C. *Ringneck: Pheasants & Pheasant Hunting.* New York, Crown, 1975. $8.95.

Knap, Jerome J. *Where to Fish & Hunt in North America.* New York, Pagurian Press, 1974. $8.95.

Merrill, William K. *Hunter's Bible.* New York, Doubleday, 1968. $2.50.

O'Connor, Jack. *Complete Book of Shooting: Rifles, Shotguns, Handguns.* New York, Harper & Row, 1965. $8.95.

Osmond, Clyde. *Small Game Hunting.* New York, Barnes & Noble, 1974. $1.95.

Sell, Francis. *Art of Small Game Hunting.* Harrisburg, Pa., Stackpole, 1973. $3.95.

Taylor, Zack. *Successful Waterfowling.* New York, Crown, 1974. $8.95.

Trefethen, J. *New Hunter's Encyclopedia.* Philadelphia, Quality Books, 1972. $12.98.

Waterman, Charles F. *Hunting Upland Birds.* South Hackensack, N.J., Stoeger, 1975. $5.95.

Magazines:

Field & Stream. Monthly. CBS Publications, 383 Madison Avenue, New York 10017. $7.95 per year.

Fur-Fish-Game. Monthly. A. R. Harding Publishing Co., 2878 East Main Street, Columbus, Oh. 43209. $4.00 per year.

Sports Afield. Monthly. Hearst Corp., 250 West 55th Street, New York 10019. $7.00 per year.

8 *Fishing*

G ONE FISHING," a sign on the door not uncommon in the old days of storekeeping, conjured up in one's mind a scene of perfect contentment and enjoyment. The bamboo pole, cork, string, fishing hook, and weight—that's all the equipment one needed to head for the creek and, with a worm on the hook, try for bullheads. I don't know if there are many fishing holes left on the small streams in rural America. The ones I knew as a youngster no longer exist, I'm sure.

It is still possible, with just such simple gear, to enjoy fishing. Nowadays, however, one is likely to be fishing from a small boat on a lake, probably not for bullheads but for panfish—crappies, sunfish, and bluegills. Everyone should enjoy the leisurely pursuit of fish. It is a prescription guaranteed to cure many infirmities. Small wonder that more people enjoy fishing than almost any other recreational activity.

Fishing, of course, doesn't appeal to everyone, often perhaps because they do not become sufficiently experienced to fully appreciate it. Washington Irving apparently was one who gave it up almost from the start. He wrote:

> For my part, I was always a bungler at all kinds of sport that required either patience or adroitness, and had not angled for above half an hour before I had completely "satisfied that sentiment," and convinced myself of the truth of Izaak Walton's opinion, that angling is something like poetry—a man must be born to it. I hooked myself instead of the fish; tangled my line in every tree; lost my bait; broke my rod; until I gave up the attempt to despair.

Izaak Walton, in *The Compleat Angler*, asserts that fishing is an art, for as he says, "Is it not an art to deceive a trout with an artificial fly—a trout that is more sharp-sighted than any hawk and more watchful and timorous than your high-mettled falcon is bold?" He further states:

> he that hopes to be a good angler must not only bring an inquiring, searching, observing wit, but he must also bring a large measure of hope and patience and a love and propensity for the art itself. But having once got and practiced it, then doubt not but angling will prove to be so pleasant that it will prove to be like virtue, a reward to itself.

I don't recall any President who has been particularly interested in fishing. It was surprising to learn during a recent visit to the Herbert Hoover Library at West Branch, Iowa, that he apparently liked to fish. There is a placard in the library that carries this quotation from the President:

'Tis the chance to wash one's soul with pure air, with a rush of the brook, or with the shimmer of the sun on the blue water. It brings meekness and inspiration from the decency of nature, charity toward fish, a mockery of profits and egos, a quieting of hate, a rejoicing that you do not have to decide a darned thing until next week. And it is discipline in the equality of men, for all men are equal before fish.

Herbert Hoover

Through the years I have had opportunities to enjoy various fishing experiences. Several times we fished for walleyed pike on Lake of the Woods, a beautiful, mammoth inland lake above the Minnesota-Canada border. We established headquarters at Sioux Narrows, Ontario. Early in the morning on a typical outing, we would meet our guide at the dock. He had the boat equipped with bait, life jackets, preparations for shore lunch, and landing nets. We brought our own tackle, clothes for warmth or rain, and a cooler for refreshments. As soon as the morning fog lifted, we settled down in the boat for a ride of 20 or more miles. It took us around the myriad islands which make this such a beautiful lake. We headed for the best fishing spots known to the guide.

The trip by boat through this lake is, in itself, so enjoyable that the actual fishing becomes a bonus. Dodging rocky shoals here and there, our skilled boatsman finally edged into a sheltered bay. We got ready for action, following his advice on what bait to use. Live minnows is the typical bait for walleye. Then back and forth we would troll, each of us hoping to catch the first, or the largest fish. The guide also fished and, not surprisingly, he usually caught the first one. His own success largely determined whether he had chosen a good site. If no one was catching fish within 10 minutes, he moved on to another location.

Walleyed pike are not the easiest fish to catch. They nudge the bait, sometimes nimbly taking it into their mouths as if they are sucking on it. Generally, one does not get a clear signal that they are taking it. In fact, if you get a strong signal you can predict that you have something else, such as a perch, bass, or northern pike, playing your bait. The guide will let you miss one or two, but then he will give you pointers on how to determine the right time to set the hook. Soon you will be catching fish and then *you* are hooked! You experience the thrill that brings fishermen back again and again to this marvelous sport.

Fishing, more than most sports, has many spin-off enjoyments. I've mentioned the boat trip through beautiful scenery as one. In an

outing such as I have just described, there is the camaraderie of your fishing companions, as well as the competition. But the shore lunch which the guide prepares is the highlight of the day. First, some of the fish caught during the morning are cleaned. (I'm not sure why that term is commonly used.) Then, in a make-shift fireplace of rocks, the water, coffee, a frying pan with potatoes, and a pan with lots of butter for the fish are placed on the grill. The guide fills the pan with what appears to be fish enough for twice your number. Never will you taste more delicious fish than these. All the fish you can eat, and that will be more than you thought you could.

You arrive back at camp about sundown. Chances are you caught your limit of walleyes. The guide completes his service by cleaning them for you, wrapping and freezing them ready for you to take home.

Recently, I accompanied my son fishing for trout in the Frying Pan River in central Colorado. It is one of the beautiful streams that make fishing so enjoyable. I had never experienced trout fishing before. That day I took pictures of son Tom and observed the art of flycasting. He is enthusiastic about the sport, and I now understand why. "You are conscious of the beauty, excitement, and ever-present sound of rushing water," he said.

An Orvis Flycasting School instructor helps a young pupil.

The rest of the world becomes distant. There is only you, the stream, and the fish that you know are down there but only occasionally see. You cast your dry fly, the most popular type. It floats ever so gently on the surface of the water. Then you watch the current taking it along and splash! It disappears and you find yourself playing a rainbow trout. Because of the light tackle you use, it seems much larger than it is.

Anyone who has never fly-fished has missed a great way to spend a day. It is in many ways unique. There are many avid followers of this sport, and for good reason.

Needless to say someday I'll go back and try my own luck.

Several years ago my wife and I, accompanied by a few friends, chartered a boat at Westport, Washington, and fished for salmon off the Pacific coast. There were 7 of us in addition to the skipper. Since deep sea fishing requires special tackle, it was furnished with the boat. Boats used for such outings are equipped with the comforts of home, with galley, head, and bunks. Lunch is prepared in advance and eaten on board, although the skipper did fry a few of the fish we caught, just for the novelty of it.

We had an unusually successful day. We all caught our limit of 3 salmon each. In addition, we caught many sea bass which mostly were thrown back in. This, for a small lake fisherman like myself, was shocking, especially since there were bass larger than I had ever caught in my life in Wisconsin. We did convince the skipper to keep a few, which eventually we brought back home with us. The fins on sea bass, however, are treacherous and we almost regretted having to cope with them as we packed our fish for the return home.

In arranging for this fishing venture we scheduled our return flight for the morning after our outing. Fortunately, we were able to bring our 6 salmon back as regular baggage. They were packed in ice and placed in styrofoam boxes when we returned to the dock. This kept them beautifully until we got home and placed them in our freezer. We probably had over 50 pounds of fresh salmon which we proudly served, freshly broiled over a charcoal grill, to many of our friends at successive dinner parties.

Deep sea fishing is not just an ordinary fishing experience. A few years ago I was with a group that chartered a boat at Miami, Florida, and fished some 30 miles off the east coast. The fellowship, fun, and laughter of the group added greatly to the enjoyment of fishing. All equipment was furnished, and the guide baited the hooks and helped land the fish caught. The only real fishing activity the individual guests did was to reel in the fish. However, there was the usual excitement when someone caught a big one, such as a tuna. For someone reared in land-locked mid-America, deep sea fishing is a rare treat.

For those of us in the midwest, the finest, most desirable fish to catch is the walleyed pike. Several times my wife and I have taken our 14-foot boat up to Leech Lake, the largest lake in Minnesota. Leech Lake has the reputation as one of the finest walleye fishing lakes in this state if not anywhere. Despite the fact that our luck was not good, these excursions were memorable events. We packed a picnic lunch and headed to the favored spots some 15 miles out from shore. In comfortable seats, with a top shading us from the bright sun, we worked the holes, enjoying the absolute peace and quiet of the open lake. These trips illustrated so very well that the enjoyment of fishing includes the beautiful environment, the solitude, the setting aside of all cares and worries, and the companionship of one's wife or husband or friends.

As I describe in the chapter on canoeing, I have enjoyed a number of canoe trips in the Quetico–Superior National Forest. Fishing on such trips is an indispensable activity. Indispensable in that fish is planned as part of the week's menu. Since all food is packed in with you, and since meat and eggs will keep safely for only a couple of days, catching fish is essential. This fact provides an added incentive to fishing. Mostly, we catch northern pike and an occasional bass. In these relatively primitive areas, fishing is generally very good. It is likely that the fish will be large and vigorous. The water is cold and freshly caught fish is especially delicious cooked over the campfire.

I am a patient fisherman. There is no discouragement for me in fishing for one or two hours and not catching a fish. There is so much to enjoy while fishing on our Wisconsin lakes. The marshes are alive with wildlife in their natural habitat. Turtles are sunning themselves on the floating bogs, a blue heron rises overhead in awkward flight, loons cry out to each other from one end of the lake to the other, ducks flutter and streak skyward, a muskrat expresses surprise as he rounds a weed clump and discovers a boat in his territory, and the air reverberates with the croaking of bullfrogs. The water is so clear that one can see thousands of small fishes playing below and around the boat.

The chief benefit of fishing, which appears to be universally accepted, is its power to lift the spirit, calm and soothe the nerves, to absorb completely our attention and thinking, to block out the cares of the world, and bring us into harmony with nature. Fishing has a marvelous therapeutic effect on a person who has been facing the stresses of the job and the fast pace of life as it is typically lived today. The one dominant desire I have in early spring, as the snow melts and the ice thaws on the lakes, is to get out my boat and go fishing.

There are thousands who are not only warm-water fishermen but also ice fishermen. This sport is for the hardy unless, as is increasingly the case, you are among those who take ice fishing seriously and participate in the colonies established on lakes in the northern U.S. These groups build well-equipped, heated, and stocked fishing houses with many of the comforts of home, including television sets, bars, and cooking facilities. Fishing can be done through a hole in the floor, with signals attached to the fishing equipment to alert the fishermen when they have a nibble. For those who have lake cabins, ice fishing is relatively simple. All that is required is to drill a hole in the ice a reasonable distance off shore, in sight of the cabin. By placing a signal device, including a small light, on the tackle, one can see from the cabin when a fish has been hooked.

FUNDAMENTALS OF FISHING.   For those who have never fished, the sport is quite simple. It can easily be learned, it is inexpensive, and the rewards are great. It consists, in its simplest concept, of offering fish the food they want, at a time they want to eat. To accomplish this, one must make everything appear as natural as possible. Tackle manufacturers go to great lengths to develop virtually invisible lines and to make artificial lures look like natural food.

The art of fishing includes knowing where the fish are and when they are eating. Every fish has its own eating habits, and one has to become familiar with what they like and when. Each species must also be landed in a certain way. For example, bullheads jerk the line with a definite force, sinking the bobber. The walleye nibble or bump the bait so softly that one has to remain alert so as not to miss it. A northern pike will take the line and head for the deep waters with great force and speed. A largemouth bass will leap a foot or more out of the water in an attempt to eject the lure from his mouth. Each fish presents a different situation to the fisherman trying to land it.

EQUIPMENT NEEDED.   Assembling fishing tackle sometimes appears to be an end in itself. It is something fishermen seem very much to enjoy doing. The variety of plugs and other artificial lures available gives rise to comments such as, "The manufacturers have designed these more to catch fishermen than fish." In all candor I suspect there is some validity to the assertion. Some fishermen may be attracted by new designs of plugs. Experienced sportsmen often know what works in the area they fish and tend to stick to proven lures. I am pretty much a one-plug fisherman and know that over the years my Grey Mouse lure has caught more fish for me than any other lure I might use. In fact, I've made quite a few converts by demonstrating the effectiveness of this plug.

Fishing tackle can be relatively simple and reasonable in cost, or it can be elaborate and expensive. It all depends upon the tastes and interests of the fisherman. Leaving deep sea fishing aside, small tackle consists basically of a rod, reel, line, lures, and a landing net. One can add a number of useful items to this basic list, such as stringers or a holding net to contain the fish after they are caught, and a tackle box to hold the various weights, lures, leaders, lines, hooks, reel oil, bobbers, and other tackle. The first important decision that has to be made is what kind of fish, in general, you will be fishing for. From that will flow other decisions as to the types of reel, rod, and line.

For the casual recreational fisherman there are 3 basic reels. The *casting* reel is an all-purpose fishing reel. It basically is a spool that revolves as you cast out the line. The *spinning* reel is the simplest to operate, and therefore a favorite of many beginners, as well as some experienced fishermen. Contrary to its name, the spool is stationary when the line is cast out, with the line playing off the end of the spool. The third is the reel used for fly-fishing.

Reels, whether casting or spinning types, are perhaps the most important part of your fishing tackle. It is better to buy a good reel and economize on other parts of the equipment, for a reel that

A fly-tying class in progress

doesn't perform well can be frustrating, the last thing a beginning fisherman needs. One should expect to invest $35 or more in a good reel. The other tackle is likely to cost upwards of $100 by the time it is all assembled.

Fly-fishing equipment costs are similar to those of other rods and reels. Fly fishing also requires a few extra items such as waders and a creel in which the trout are placed when caught. The creel is a basket-like container carried by a shoulder strap. Also, since the fly fisherman fishes from the middle of the stream, he must have a carrier for his various lures and other items he needs so that he doesn't have to return to shore each time he makes a catch.

Fly-tying is a special kind of activity for the fly fisherman. Many people are as enthusiastic about tying flies as they are about fishing. It can be an absorbing hobby in itself. Tying your own flies makes the cost of the individual fly, which tends to be expendable in the fishing process, very low—a few cents perhaps. Ready-made flies are much more expensive. As son Tom, who makes all his own flies, expressed it, "This may seem like an art only for a skilled craftsman, but even a novice can tie a respectable fly. He needs only a small amount of instruction, from books available on the technique. And the payoff is the great feeling you have when you catch a fish with a fly that you created." Some sporting goods stores and adult education programs offer instruction in fly-tying at little or no cost.

LOCATION OF FISHING SITES. Where to fish should not be a difficult problem for most people, unless they live in arid areas. Each state has public information on fishing areas. Contact the state tourist bureau or the department of natural resources for information. They can provide license requirements, maps, resort guides, season dates, and regulations on fishing. Most states have two fee schedules for licenses, one for residents and one for nonresidents. For nonresidents there typically is a license that can be obtained for brief periods of 3 days or a week, as well as the season license. Unfortunately, many states have nonresident fees so high that it discourages roving from one state to another for fishing. This is too bad for those who like to go on camping vacations. The freedom to fish without exorbitant additional costs would add much to the camping experience. Some states have waived the license requirement for those over 65 years old, so if you fall in that category, it is worth inquiring. Often, however, this applies only to the state in which you have your legal residence.

TIPS FOR OLDER FISHERMEN. If you have never fished to speak of in your life and admit not knowing much about it, by all

A surf caster extends his forearm to complete the cast. Waders allow you to cast farther out. Note the rod holder in the background.

means begin by going out with someone who can show you some of the basics. If you have no friends who are fishermen, then arrange for a day with a guide at a fishing resort. Not only will you have an enjoyable outing, you will learn techniques that you will be able to apply when you go out alone. Often I observe novice fishermen on the lake in front of our cabin in Wisconsin. I often think of what a friend of mine told me once when I was fishing in the middle of a lake, pretty much at random as far as location is concerned. He said "you might as well stay home and fish in your bath tub." Fish can make humble people out of the greatest among us. Therefore, it is advisable to take a little advice from someone who has been humbled, and later learned to match wits with the fish.

One of the common reactions when one catches a large fish is excitement. It is at this moment that one must observe precautions. It is tempting to stand up in the boat. If you are not alone, other occupants of the boat may want to see the action and all lean on the same

side. Keep your cool and don't bring disaster out of triumph by up-
setting the boat, or falling out of it. Some fishermen like to cast out
their line from a standing position. Don't! Unless, of course, you are
in a fishing launch with a fishing party and guide. Small, lightweight,
shallow aluminum fishing boats simply are not designed for stand-up
fishing. To do so is to invite trouble.

After you have learned the basics of fishing, try fishing alone. It
is a sport that offers a meditative experience unmatched by any
other. Of course it is fun to have company in the boat too, but fishing alone is a special kind of treat. Wear a life jacket to remove any
danger or apprehension you may have about falling in the water.
Then relax! Sometimes I wish I smoked a pipe, for a pipe-smoking
fisherman alone in a boat, fishing with a hook and bobber, is the perfect picture of tranquility.

Although catching fish is the primary objective of going fishing
there are certainly a number of enjoyable by-products. Therefore,
even if you have caught very few fish, you can shift your attention to
these by-products. Just being out on the water early in the morning
before the sun rises, listening to the birds in the nearby woods, or
watching the muskrat or beaver or ducks swim across the lake, can
render the actual fishing process secondary. How beautiful is a
golden sunset when viewed from a boat on a lake! The croaking of
bullfrogs, or the call of the loon, or the flight of the blue heron—

what thrilling experiences these are in contrast to our normal, noisy, turbulent work-a-day world.

Fishing from a rowboat is preferable to using a noisy motor but, of course, harder work if one must go some distance to the fishing spot. If you do use a motor don't go roaring into the place you want to fish and expect the fish to remain there undisturbed. You've already nearly blown your chances of catching anything if you do. One of the attractive ways of fishing is by using the small inexpensive electric trolling motors now available. They are very nearly soundless and are less disturbing even than rowing the boat. They are not designed to cover long distances, but they offer an attractive alternative once one arrives at the fishing spot to be worked.

If you have arrived at 50 years old or older and have never fished, you are unique. An estimated 53.9 million people over 9 years old are recreational fishermen, according to a 1975 U.S. Fish and Wildlife Service survey. Of these fishermen 69 percent are male and 31 percent female, and they together spent $15.2 billion for fishing activities in 1975. They *valued* their fishing experiences at $154.5 billion!

FOR MORE INFORMATION

There are many publications on fishing, attesting to the popularity of the sport. I have listed some that will provide interesting reading and much more detailed information than I have given. There are, in addition, books on regional fishing, and I have listed several titles as examples. A visit to your local public library or bookstore will show you the wide array of books and magazines available.

Books:

Allyn, Rube. *A Dictionary of Fishes.* St. Petersburg, Fl., Great Outdoors Publishing Co., 1976. $1.95.
An excellent guide for the identification of some 700 species of fish. Description includes the Latin name, size, edibility, color, characteristics, habitat, and food. Illustrations in color and black and white.
——. *Fisherman's Handbook.* St. Petersburg, Fl., Great Outdoors Publishing Co., 1962. $1.00.
A well-illustrated, inexpensive guide useful for beginners interested in learning the principles of fishing for various species of fish, including bass, trout, crab, grouper, lobster, and game salt water fish.
Boyd, Lester C. *Atlantic Surf Fishing: Maine to Maryland.* Boston, Stone Wall Press, 1976. $4.95.
A book of personal testimony on the fun of surf fishing on the eastern shores. Describes tackle required, good fishing spots, and the species of fish in different areas.
Chiapetta, Jerry. *Ice Fishing.* Harrisburg, Pa., Stackpole, 1975. $3.95.
A good guide to this increasingly popular type of fishing. It includes a directory of ice fishing locations.

Noll, H. J. *Noll Guide to Trout Flies and How to Tie Them.* New York, Davis-Delaney-Arrow, 1970.

An excellent guide, beautifully illustrated by G. Don Ray.

Ovington, Ray. *Basic Fly Fishing & Fly-Tying.* Harrisburg, Pa., Stackpole, 1973. $3.95.

For the beginner in fly fishing. Drawings assist the reader in the art of fly-tying, rigging the tackle, and placing the fly in various fishing situations.

Smith, A. Paul. *How to Fish for Bass.* St. Petersburg; Fl., Great Outdoors Publishing Co., 1967. $1.00.

Simple, direct, and well illustrated. Concentrates on bass only. Includes a guide to the best bass fishing spots in Florida.

Sosin, Mark, ed. *Angler's Bible.* Chicago, Follett, 1975. $7.95.

The combination of bedtime reading and dictionary of tackle, with specifications, makes this an interesting addition to a fishing library. Included is a comprehensive listing of books on fishing and a directory of magazines of interest to the angler, as well as other useful reference information.

Magazines:

Bassmaster Magazine. Bi-monthly. Bass Anglers Sportsman Society of America, Inc., P.O. Box 3044, Montgomery, Al. $7.00 per year.

Field & Stream. Monthly, CBS Publications, Inc., 383 Madison Ave., New York 10017. $7.95 per year.

Fishing Facts. Monthly. Northwoods Publishing Co., Inc., Box 609, Menomonee Falls, Wi. 53051. $12.00 per year.

Fly Fisherman. 7 issues per year. Box 10002, Des Moines, Ia. 50340. $10.00 per year.

Fur-Fish-Game. Monthly. Harding Publishing Co., 2878 East Main St., Columbus, Oh. 43209. $5.00 per year.

Sports Afield. Monthly. Hearst Corp., 250 West 55th St., New York. $7.00 per year.

Sports & Recreation. Bi-monthly. 9100 Cottonwood Lane, Maple Grove, Minn. 55369. $3.50 per year.

An example of a regional publication. This focuses on Minnesota–Wisconsin.

9 *Swimming*

I T IS A beautiful experience to watch an expert swimmer gracefully dive into the pool and smoothly reach the other end. Lucky is the person who grew up with swimming as a normal sports activity. Youngsters always seem to have so much fun in the water and that enjoyment, learned at an early age, carries throughout one's lifetime. It is easy to distinguish those who have always swum from those, like myself, who learned to swim as adults. We never seem quite as comfortable or natural in the water. One can tell by the reluctance we show in diving into a lake or pool.

Age, in itself, is no deterrent to the enjoyment of swimming. My former neighbor at our lake cabin rarely missed a day of swimming in the lake, from early spring to late fall, even when the water was cold. He would dive off the board, swim around, climb up on the dock and dive again, repeatedly, perhaps several times a day when the weather was hot. He was in his early 90's. Only a few years earlier, when well into his 80's, he would ride the aquaplane around the lake behind his son's boat. His family grew up enjoying the water and some of them think nothing of swimming across the lake and back, a distance of about ½ mile.

It is surprising that more older people do not swim. It is an activity that has many advantages over other sports. It is recognized as one of the best ways of gaining physical fitness. Swimming facilities are available in many places, from public pools to private home pools. Increasingly, school swimming pools are being made accessible to communities at certain scheduled hours, at very little cost. YMCA's and other similar organizations have pools available to members. When you are traveling, motels and hotels often provide swimming facilities (though some, to be sure, are not much more than glorified wading pools). In areas where there are lakes there are almost limitless opportunities for swimming. Despite this, it is estimated that only 4 percent of Americans over 60 swim.

Swimming also has the distinct advantage of low cost. Often the swimsuit is the only expense. For women this may not be an incidental expense, especially if they want the latest style every year. But compared to such activities as golf or downhill skiing, swimming is indeed very inexpensive.

One aspect of swimming is especially appealing to those of us who never swam competitively. It is a sport that lets you pace yourself, without regard to anyone else. You can set up your own objective of as many laps as you may want to swim, within whatever time you wish. There are no points or scores to be made, only fun and good physical exercise.

It is surprising how much exertion swimming requires. Of course, it depends on one's ability and the speed one swims. But in the table reprinted in Chapter 2, you can see that swimming the breast stroke at 40 yards per minute is equivalent to climbing stairs or running 5.5 miles per hour. Swimming the crawl stroke is likened to heavy labor. For this reason swimming is recognized as one of the good conditioning activities to achieve physical fitness, along with jogging and bicycling. Swimming is one of the few sports that, rather than causing sore muscles, actually is a therapy prescribed by doctors for conditioning after some accidents or surgery. However, if fitness is the objective in your swimming, it requires more than lolling around in the water. For physical conditioning you should set up a program of swimming that builds up your capacity for oxygen intake. Such a program should follow the regimen prescribed by books on fitness such as those by Dr. Kenneth Cooper. Books written about swimming often do not dwell on this aspect of the sport, but focus more on its competitive aspects, such as muscle building, strategy, technique, and attitude.

One of the most unusual swimming experiences we had was at a little-known place called Pamukkale in southwest Turkey. Here, hot, calcium-laden waters with a high carbon dioxide content emerge from the earth. Over the years deposits from these waters have created terraces behind which the water forms pools. One of these pools covers the ruins of the old Biblical city of Hierapolis. Aside from the health benefits one reputedly gains from swimming in these springs, one has the fascinating experience of floating over and around old Greek columns and capitals in unbelievably crystal clear water.

We who have attained the "age of maturity" doubtless have recollections of swimming in various places over the years. Keeping a tally can in itself be a challenge, similar to the game some people play of visiting every state in the United States. For my part, without establishing any objectives along this line, I already have swum in the Atlantic and Pacific Oceans, the Gulf of Mexico, the Mediterranean, Aegean, and Adriatic Seas, in a lake in Finland following an authentic sauna, in a Turkish bath, and in the Dead Sea. Regrettably, I have no recollection of having skinny-dipped in the moonlight, but any bona fide canoer has swum in the raw.

Safety is an understandable concern for older people when swimming. It is less of a problem when swimming in pools at the YWCA or a local high school. Municipal pools or lakes with swimming beaches that are patrolled by lifeguards present little risk, even for those who may not know how to swim very well. The drownings that do occur (and the percentage of those swimming who drown is very low), are more likely to happen in lakes where there are few other people around. In fact, drowning accidents are mostly associated with boating, not swimming. Swimming accidents *per se* are very infrequent.

One way that my wife and I avoid the risks of swimming when we are in our lake alone is to wear safety belts. These are just buoyant enough to keep one afloat but not so bulky as to prevent one from enjoying swimming. In fact, we prefer wearing them not for safety's sake alone but because they enable us to venture out in the deep areas of the lake and bask in the sun without having to constantly paddle our legs and arms to remain afloat. If we wish to swim any distance we move much more easily without the belts, of course, since they do drag against the water. Inner tubes are commonly used as flotation devices, but they are very unwieldy. On the market also are many other items ranging from plastic air mattresses to lounge-like inflated rafts.

Learning to swim requires following definite techniques and a great deal of practice. Coordination of breathing and arm strokes appears simple but is difficult to learn. That I know from personal experience. Once you learn how, however, it requires much less effort to swim. Endurance, I am convinced, is not so much a matter of fitness—although that is vital—as it is technique. Therefore, if at all possible, one should obtain swimming instruction. Chances are that your local community education offerings include swimming. Also, YM–YWCA's and other similar organizations usually offer swimming lessons and make their pools available to members.

One of the encouraging developments nationally is the attention our government is giving to both physical fitness programs and senior citizen activities. The next few years will see much more government assistance for fitness and activities programs in social service agencies, schools, and municipalities. High schools and colleges are offering their facilities to older people also. Swimming instruction, therefore, should become increasingly available for those wishing to develop or improve their technique.

TIPS FOR OLDER SWIMMERS. At our lake cabin we seldom can get older friends to put on their bathing suits and get in the water. When they do they inevitably enjoy it. Why the great reluctance? Could it be that older people don't like to be seen in bathing suits? Do their figures embarrass them? Do they associate swimming with frolicking in the water and do they feel they are beyond the frolicking stage? Is it the lack of competition in swimming that makes it uninteresting for them? Why is it that only 4 percent of those over 60 swim?

Home swimming pools are too expensive for most people and are somewhat bothersome to maintain. Otherwise they would appear to be an answer for those who find difficulty in swimming because of lack of accessibility of facilities, public exposure in swimming suits, or hesitation about frolicking in a public pool. The home pool also lends itself to social events, becoming a center of focus for parties. But because of their high costs and space requirements, home pools can be the answer for only a small percentage of people. They are not apt to increase in any substantial way the number of older people who will participate in the sport of swimming.

When one hears about the physical benefits of swimming it would seem that much more attention would be paid to this sport. One of the things that is missing, I suspect, is emphasis on the "fun" factor in swimming. There is a therapy in swimming not found in many sports. Mention was made of the beneficial results of swimming for the relief of sore muscles. It is often prescribed as a rehabilitative technique in some medical procedures. It is a pleasant method of maintaining muscle tone. If one follows a regimen that results in aerobic improvement, it can be one of the best fitness activities.

Aside from the physical benefits there are those who derive mental relaxation and psychological benefits from swimming. A family friend of ours, in her 50's, swims several times a week, winter and summer, in the YWCA pool, and finds that missing one or more sessions has a definite deleterious effect on her feeling of well-being.

Age has a lesser effect on one's ability to swim than it does on many other sports. Frank Gibson, of San Francisco, nearly 90 years old, reportedly swims a couple of miles a day. As a member of the South End Rowing Club, he and some of his fellow members, all over 60, swim in the San Francisco Bay, even in winter when temperatures can be in the 40's. They have swum from Alcatraz Island to the mainland, some many times. While this is an unusual group, the fact is that age does not need to ground you, and swimming can continue to be fun and healthful throughout one's lifetime.

Swimming can be one of the best activities for the control and relief of stress. Most physical exercise is helpful in this regard but swimming is certainly among the most effective. Gerald Ford and John F. Kennedy both swam regularly while they were president, and attested to the beneficial results derived from this activity.

FOR MORE INFORMATION

Unlike most animals, man does not swim naturally and has to learn how. Personal instruction from qualified teachers is the best way to learn. Reading books, preferably elementary ones geared for Boy Scouts or schools, can be a good start. There do not appear to be many books that exult over the joys of swimming. Most of them focus on teaching youngsters how to swim, or are concerned with swimming as a competitive sport. Perhaps that is all that is needed, for if one follows the directions on how to swim, the joy of swimming will become apparent as a by-product. Following are a few titles representative of the types of books available in your local bookstore or public library.

Groscost, Joseph. *Basic Swimming Guide.* New Ed. Cleveland, World Publications, 1975. $2.50.

Horn, Bob. *Swimming Techniques in Pictures.* New York, Grossett & Dunlap, 1974. $2.95.

Jarvis, Margaret. *Enjoy Swimming.* Levittown, N.Y., Transatlantic, 1972. $9.95.

Kreen, Mike. *Learn to Swim.* New York, Rand McNally, 1976. $1.95.

Law, Donald. *Beginner's Guide to Swimming & Water Sports.* New York, Drake, 1975. $4.95.

McAllister, Evelyn D. *Easy Steps to Safe Swimming.* 4th Ed. New York, Barnes & Noble, 1970. $1.50.

Mackenzie, Marlin, and Betty Spears. *Beginning Swimming.* Rev. Ed. Belmont, Ca., Wadsworth, 1974. $2.95.

Roy, Harcourt. *Beginner's Guide to Swimming & Water Safety.* New York, Drake, 1973. $5.95.

Schollander, Don, and Joel H. Cohen. *Inside Swimming.* Chicago, Regnery, 1974. $4.95.

10   *Boating*

AS THE WINTER wanes, and the warm sun of spring melts away the snow, my fancy turns not to love (sigh!) but to my boat. It is not a pretentious boat at all, not a beautiful lake cruiser with all the comforts of home. It is a simple, unadorned 14-foot aluminum fishing boat leaning against a tree on shore by our lake cottage. Anxiously I await the thawing of the ice on the lake, which occurs in mid-April in this northern area. Then at the first opportunity I will attach my small outboard motor and my wife and I will cruise around the entire lake shore to see what changes the winter has wrought.

One of our annual rituals, usually on a warm, quiet May morning, is to explore some of the less accessible parts of the lake. We watch the turtles sunning themselves on clumps of lily roots and bog. We listen to the bullfrogs croaking, and the loons calling out to their mates across the lake. Teals and blue herons rise to the sky as we round the bend in the bay. Muskrats swim and dive before us as we quietly meander to and fro among the reeds and rushes. We note the presence of beavers who worked against impossible odds to dam up the channel between two lakes.

One of the sights that never ceases to enchant us is the underwater life which we can observe as we enter shallow parts of the lake. Stopping the motor we let the wind push the boat quietly across the surface. The crystal clear, undisturbed water affords a glimpse of the wonderland below us. On such a quiet, sunny day we can see several feet beneath the surface. Small fishes by the thousands, and occasionally a large pike, swim about unmolested right beneath us.

In this setting we are surrounded by the attractions and sounds of nature. Birds in the adjoining woods are singing their hearts out. As we sit quietly in the warm sun, thawing out from the depression of winter, the world becomes alive with indescribable vitality. There is such an uplifting of the spirit, such a rebirth of optimism and joy! It is a therapy unavailable in prescriptions. It is the miracle of spring. Quietly I may slouch down in the bottom of the boat and lean back against the seat, letting the warm sun revitalize my being. I will close my eyes and listen. Peace! Peace! This is *my* church, my communing with God.

The boat plays a vital role in this event. It is the vehicle that provides the isolation necessary for the proper enjoyment of nature. The canoe does it even better, since it moves along silently without disturbing the wildlife about. One summer in the Boundary Waters Canoe Area at the Minnesota–Canada border, I was able to stealthily glide up to a beaver sunning himself on shore. For several long minutes I studied this magnificent animal at close range in his natural surroundings. Suddenly, he opened his eyes and plunged into the water, surfacing some 20 feet away. He then slapped his broad flat tail against the water with a clap that echoed like a gunshot across the lake. He was warning his family and friends that there was an intruder thereabouts. Then he disappeared beneath the surface and was gone.

Motor boating, as an inland lake activity, is generally associated with a companion sport, such as fishing or waterskiing. On a river, however, there is considerable enjoyment in simply cruising where one can enjoy a constant change in scenery, and where picnicking, on board or on shore, can be a delightful experience.

The range of boats available is clear evidence that this sport has become one of the nation's most popular forms of recreation. The National Association of Engine and Boat Manufacturers recently estimated that there are 50.5 million recreational boaters in the United States, with 1.8 million newcomers to boating in the last year. There are over 10 million boats in use today, up 365,000 from a year ago. Boats with inboard motors comprise the fastest growing segment of the industry, indicating that the trend appears to be to larger boats.

Recently I visited a boat show, typical of those held annually in late winter or early spring in many of the larger cities. The array of water equipment was mind-boggling. The displays, of course, are geared to the waterways in that particular area. This show was in Chicago and featured large cruisers suitable for the Great Lakes.

If one lives in a part of the country where there are lakes, the highways on Friday afternoons and evenings will provide indisputable evidence of the popularity of boating. There are caravans of cars pulling runabouts and utility boats, heading for the shores. Many cars will be carrying the increasingly popular canoes. Some will be pulling small sailboats, and a few will be trailering pontoons.

TYPES OF BOATS AVAILABLE.   There are many classes and types of boats. For purposes here we will not concern ourselves with the large lake cruisers, yachts, or motor sailers, but rather with more moderate priced recreational models. It takes considerable experience to describe some of the activities associated with larger boats, and my background has been limited to fishing from launches, seagoing sports cruisers, and day cruisers.

Judging from my experience and what I have seen at boat shows, the most prevalent boat appears to be the runabout. Typically this is a boat 14 to 20 feet long, powered by either an inboard or outboard motor. It can be used for waterskiing, fishing, or simply cruising. It is made of wood, fiber glass, or aluminum, and can be loaded or unloaded from a trailer very simply by one or two people. It is easily transportable in this way from one body of water to another or to and from storage.

The canoe is a popular favorite among more and more outdoorsmen. A normal-sized canoe, 15 to 17 feet long, weighs less than 100 pounds and can be carried on top of a car, loaded and unloaded quite simply, and launched anywhere. It is low cost to purchase and is virtually maintenance free. Since operation is by manpower, it takes no fuel. It is highly maneuverable and can be paddled into swamps and back lakes not navigable by other boating equipment. For this reason it is the only means of access, except by plane, to some of the remote lakes in the northwoods, like those in Minnesota and Canada. Canoes are made of aluminum, fiber glass, or some of the new shock-resistant plastics.

The pontoon boat is becoming more prevalent on lakes where people own cottages. Such boats are typically kept in such lakes all summer long, moored at docks in front of their owners' cottages. Typically they are made of 2 pontoons bridged by a platform or deck surrounded by a railing and powered with a small outboard motor. Some are equipped with awnings, and when folding chairs are placed on the deck, the boat can be used for picnicking, fishing, or slow cruising around the lake. It is a favorite with older people because of the safety and comfort it affords.

The boat most used by fishermen in small lakes is the utility boat. It is typically 12 to 14 feet long, made of wood, fiber glass, or aluminum, and can be rowed or powered by a small outboard motor. It is a stripped-down runabout, not very comfortable, but it has definite advantages. It is lightweight and can easily be brought on shore by one person. If it is aluminum, it is weather resistant and can be left out year round without requiring painting or other maintenance. Some of the lightweight metal utility boats can be carried on top of one's car or house trailer.

Sailboats, like other boats, range in size from the small, surfboard-like, 10-foot long wood or fiber glass models suitable for one person who has to lie more or less flat on them, to ocean-going crafts weighing tons. The Alcort "Sailfish" or "Sunfish" sailboats can be carried on top of your car and easily launched in any lake. They are less suited for older persons than for youngsters. They tip easily and, in our children's experience, the sailors spent about as much time in the water as they did sailing, which they found to be half the fun. For the less adventurous among us, 12- to 15-foot sloops are better. They will carry 4 adults, in sitting position, are easily rigged, and provide for leisurely enjoyment of sailing.

On rivers and large lakes one observes an increasing number of house boats. Essentially these are the aquatic equivalent of the travel trailers so prevalent on the highways today. House boats are not geared for speed or long trips, but basically provide living quarters for one or more days while slowly cruising on water. In many especially scenic areas, such as in the Missouri Ozarks, one can rent house

boats and live on the water during one's vacation. They can be brought to shore at any desirable isolated point and used as headquarters for fishing from a small rowboat brought along for the purpose.

These are only a few of the variety of boats available. Boating has become a very large industry. Each type or class of boat has numerous variations and I can give only generalizations to whet your interest. If you want to get started in boating, a good place to begin is to visit an annual boat show in your area. You will be somewhat disappointed in the minimum attention given to small boats, but there still will be enough examples, catalogs, and exhibitors available to provide much information.

One of the major items of equipment needed for boating (except for sailing and canoeing) is the motor. Boat motors have undergone continuous development over the years until today they are fairly efficient, extremely reliable, and quite expensive. In the case of Class A boats—that is, boats less than 16 feet long—one may pay as much for the motor as for the boat. The total investment in a boat, motor, and trailer suitable for waterskiing, for example, may be as much as for some automobiles. A fishing rig, on the other hand, can be fairly modest in cost. Buying a used boat will reduce the investment. Caution is the watchword for used motors, however, unless you are quite familiar with motors and can judge their condition. If not, buy only through a reputable dealer who will guarantee the condition and performance of the motor.

Boats of different sizes have motor size ratings to match. The U.S. Coast Guard provides motor size information on a capacity rating plate that the manufacturer places inside each boat. For safety's sake the motor used should not exceed the size indicated on this plate.

There are waterway protocols that every boatman should learn. The U.S. Coast Guard in your city may offer training programs for beginners in boating at little or no cost. Water safety is becoming increasingly important with the growing traffic on lakes and rivers. There are legal requirements with respect to licensing, safety equipment (such as life vests and boat cushions), and operation that every boater must heed. Each state has strictly enforced laws that must be observed at the risk of severe penalties. These needn't be ominous, and aren't, unless one ignores them. One needs to avoid being a hazard to others as well as oneself on the water. Most regulations are based on common-sense precautions.

There are many aspects to boating that can appeal to older people. Boating can be combined with camping, with fishing, with water-skiing, and cruising. Rowing a boat or paddling a canoe is healthy exercise and also provides cost-free transportation. If one is ambitious and likes shop work, a boat-building project can be an absorbing hobby. I haven't done much more than build a deck on my wooden fishing boat, but even that gave me a sense of accomplishment and pride in the finished product.

The most ambitious building project I have seen is that of a physician friend. It is a project of mind-boggling proportions. He began a decade or more ago to build a sea-going sailboat. The project is beyond the average individual, but it illustrates a dimension in boating that appeals to some people. We all know of the tales of people building boats in basements and who then have no way of getting them out afterwards. My doctor friend built a building, later to be dismantled, around his boat. His project has been a useful counter-activity to his medical practice and, in some respects, the pursuit of the goal of completing it is as important as the final product, if not more so. For the less ambitious do-it-yourselfer there are boat kit manufacturers who will provide plans and materials. Building your boat not only will reduce its cost but will be an activity that will have its own rewards.

Maintenance is a factor to be considered in buying a boat. Formerly, when all larger boats were made of wood, the annual spring scraping and painting ritual was demanding and gave rise to the quip that the two happiest days in the boatman's life were the day he got his boat and the day he sold it. Fortunately today, boats are made of materials that require minimum maintenance. To be sure, one still can find wooden boats and these do require painting and attention to rot. Some boats, like sailboats, often have wooden decks even though the hulls may be of fiber glass or metal, and these require varnishing and other care.

WHERE TO GO BOATING. This is hardly a problem. Most lakes of any size have public access points, often with ramps to facilitate unloading and loading your boat from the trailer. For a small fee, private resorts will permit you to use their ramps. Some 50 million people, using 10 million pleasure craft, are on the water today, and facilities abound everywhere. There are, in fact, so many alluring boating areas that one cannot hope to experience more than a few of them. The Inland Waterway along the east coast, north from Florida, or the water wonderland around Seattle, or the beautiful Muskingum River in Ohio, or the St. Croix River bordering Minnesota and

Wisconsin, or any of the federally designated scenic wild rivers, or the thousands of lakes in Michigan, Wisconsin or Minnesota, or the beautiful Ozark country in Missouri—all these, and many more, provide the would-be boater with endless opportunities for enjoyment of boating.

TIPS FOR OLDER BOATERS. Boating is one of the gentlest of sports and presents few hazards. The occasional problem or accident experienced while boating is generally brought on through the boatsman's carelessness or foolishness. What is important for older people is that they take the proper precautions when they go boating. These perhaps can best be illustrated by a couple of recent near tragedies that took place on our small lake in Wisconsin.

It was a beautiful fall day, the time of year when the water had cleared of its summer algae, the trees were beginning to take on their autumn hue, and mallards and other ducks were assembling for their annual temptation of hunters. We were busily preparing for winter, readying our runabout for storage, raking leaves, splitting wood, buttoning up our cottage and draining water pipes. Suddenly we heard desperate cries for help. We dashed down to the waterfront and saw 4 people struggling in the water across the lake. Fortunately my fishing boat was alongside our dock, but without the outboard motor. No time to get that. I rowed toward the scene as fast as I could. All of the victims were past middle age, some with medical problems which exacerbated the situation. They were clinging to boat cushions and life preservers, but the water was cold and it was urgent that we get them into the boat as quickly as possible. Between my effort and that of another lake resident who had arrived with his boat, we were able to get all aboard. After depositing them at their dock nearby we assessed what had happened. They had gone boating in a small runabout, which may have been somewhat overloaded. No one in the party was wearing a life jacket. Apparently the propeller of the motor had become tangled with weeds and, in an attempt to clear it, the boat operator had reversed the motor. As the boat moved backward, water had flowed in over the transom, adding to the weight in the boat, and soon the boat simply sank. The lake was fairly shallow, so the boat ended up with the top of the deck still above water, but the motor was resting in the mud at the bottom of the lake. The moral of this incident is twofold: First, it is wise policy to wear life jackets when you are in a boat. Secondly, be careful and don't put too heavy a load in the boat, beyond its reasonable capacity.

The second incident, which also could have had a tragic outcome, happened in about the same place, in the same lake. In this case two men, father and son, were fishing. The father was over 80 years old, and still fishing, bless his heart! But if he had been fishing all of his life it was a miracle he had lived so long, considering how he was doing it. What happened was what I see far too often, and it makes me shudder each time I see it. These two men were in a small aluminum boat and standing up! Apparently, whether as a consequence of trying to land a fish, or for some other reason, one of the men lost his balance and the boat tipped over, throwing both in the water. Neither was wearing a life jacket, and it quickly became apparent that the father could not swim. How fortunate they were that the nearest lakeshore resident was standing on his dock and saw the incident. Also, as luck would have it, he was a strong swimmer, and not having a boat at hand, he swam out the 50 yards or so to the victims and brought the father to shore. The son fortunately was able to stay with the boat and came to shore on his own. The lesson to be learned here is again twofold. Older people would be well advised to wear life jackets when there is the possibility of danger. And, for heavens sake, don't ever stand up in a small boat while fishing!

FOR MORE INFORMATION

There are many books and magazines on boating. Some will guide you in buying equipment and acquainting you with boating protocol and regulations. Others will be regionally oriented. Following is a list of a few to give you examples of the range available. Check with your public library or your local bookstore. You will find these books and others available provide the many details essential for you to fully enjoy the wonderful sport of boating.

Books:
Better Boating: A Guide to Safety Afloat. 4th Ed. Seattle, Outdoor Empire Pub., 1974.
Bunker, M. *Damn the Garbage, Full Speed Ahead: An Account and Handbook on the Pleasures of Boating.* New York, McGraw-Hill, 1973. $5.95.
Engel, Lyle K. *Complete Book of Outboard Boating.* New York, Arco, 1975. $3.95.
Klein, David. *Your First Boat: How to Choose It, How to Use It.* New York, Funk & Wagnalls, 1967. $1.50.
Morris, Dan, and Inez Morris. *Camping by Boat.* Indianapolis, Bobbs-Merrill, 1975. $5.95.
Wickham, A. J., and Hilary Wickham. *Motor Boating: A Practical Handbook.* New York, Transatlantic, 1976. $5.50.
Magazines:
American Boating. Monthly. Real Resources Group, Box A, Reno, Nev. 89506. $5.00 per year.
Boating. Monthly. P.O. Box 2773, Boulder, Co. 80321. $9.00 per year.
Go Boating. Monthly. Graphic Publications, Inc., 261 SW 6th Street, Miami, Fl. 33130. $5.00 per year.

Motor Boating & Sailing. Monthly. 959 Eighth Avenue, New York 10019. $10.00 per year.

Motorboat. Monthly. 38 Commercial Wharf, Boston, Mass. 02110. $9.50 per year.

Southern Boating. Monthly. 615 SW 2nd Avenue, Miami, Fl. 33130. $6.00 per year.

Southern Waterways. Monthly. Box 1255, Fort Myers, Fl. 33902. $2.50 per year.

11 *Canoeing*

ONE OF THE earliest forms of travel in North America was by means of the forerunner of the modern-day canoe. The *voyageurs* who traversed from the St. Lawrence to the inland reaches of the continent, patterned their mode of travel after the native American Indians, who used canoes covered with birchbark. The history of this country would be considerably different had it not been for the canoe. It was the only means of transportation beyond the larger bodies of water to which the early ships were able to sail.

For the past 350 years non-Indians have been using the canoe for commerce, exploration and travel, and recreation. It still remains one of the most efficient, simple, and inexpensive means of traveling by water. And today it performs the same function of giving the canoeist access to remote areas not otherwise reachable, except perhaps by airplane. Since these areas are largely unspoiled by man, they remain precious as a last refuge from a material-burdened society.

Perhaps it is inevitable that one is given to hyperbole when describing the experience of canoeing in the Superior National Forest. It must be lived, for no description can do it justice. Words do not amply convey the depth of feeling one has while gliding smoothly and silently through pristine waters and virgin wilderness.

This beautiful forest, set aside in 1909 by President Theodore Roosevelt, comprises some 3 million acres of lakes and woods. It is adjoined, on the Canadian side of the border, by another 1600 square miles of the Quetico Provincial Park. The area, known as the Boundary Waters Canoe Area, is one of the few unspoiled outdoor recreational sites left in the United States and is protected by the U.S. government.

Years before I became a resident of Minnesota, a friend of mine described in ecstatic terms the marvels of taking canoe trips in this beautiful land. When eventually fate willed that I too came to live in Minnesota, one of the first plans I made was to experience the much-touted canoe trip. In the intervening quarter of a century, I have enjoyed several of these marvelous adventures, some with friends, some with my family. These truly are unforgettable experiences and, fortunately, are the kind that anyone at almost any age can enjoy.

Canoeing combines many of the activities I write about in this book. Paddling a canoe is a considerable amount of exercise. Camping is essential. Hiking becomes a part of the enjoyment of exploring the area where you camp. Fishing is an indispensable activity, for you depend on fish as part of the trip's food supply. One cannot but become interested in the natural wildlife and birds of the area. Swimming is a normal daily routine. And one can even rig the canoe as a sailboat.

There are, of course, many places other than the Quetico-Superior area in which canoeing can be enjoyed. Some of the rivers of the U.S. offer delightful one-day trips, or even overnight camping opportunities. For example, the Brule River at the Wisconsin-Michigan Upper Peninsula Border, or the Pine River in the Nicollet National Forest, a feeder river to the Brule River, are particularly spectacular in the fall as the autumn leaves burst out in all their splendor. One can combine river canoeing in these areas with trout fishing and camping.

If one is interested in history, canoeing is a way of reliving the experiences of the *voyageurs*, Indians, explorers, and early missionaries, by following portions of the routes from the St. Lawrence to the Mississippi River. Manitoba, Canada, has many well-mapped canoe routes in most provincial parks which follow routes first traveled and logged by naturalists and historians.

East, west, south, as well as north, each has its favorite canoeing areas. These afford pleasure and recreation for families and people of all ages. A recent issue of *Modern Maturity* tells of 84-year old Pierre Pulling, one of the world's expert canoeists, who skillfully negotiated Spring Creek on Idaho's Fort Hill Indian Reservation near Pocatello. He is one of the many older people enjoying this sport.

When I began planning my first canoe trip I was fascinated by the diary kept by one of my colleagues during a trip she had taken a year earlier. It provided an insight into this unique experience that was most helpful in my own preparations, for I had never been in the canoe country. Emulating that account is the following description which is my recollection of one such trip I took with my family. It may convey the sense of adventure, challenges, and enjoyment we experienced.

A TYPICAL CANOE TRIP

Well in advance (perhaps two months) of our vacation, we began planning for a canoe trip in the Superior National Forest in Northern Minnesota. Such advanced planning, we had learned, was essential, for we had to decide which specific routes we wanted to take. Area maps are available that provide details as to the number and difficulty of portages, the availability of campsites, and the length of a desirable circle route that provides new scenery the entire trip. Once we decided where we were going and the specific date, we wrote to a canoe outfitter in that area and reserved two canoes. Since there were 5 of us we decided on 17-foot canoes. Three of us and some gear would be in one, and the major part of the gear and two of us in the other.

Fortunately, we owned our own tent, sleeping bags, and other camping gear. And we planned on assembling all our food for the week ourselves. Outfitters can, of course, provide all requirements for canoers if they do not own their own gear. This naturally adds somewhat to the total cost of outfitting.

Since we were planning to assemble our own gear, it was essential to have a detailed checklist so as not to overlook needed items. Books on canoeing usually have such checklists that have proved useful.

Finally, the day for our adventure arrived. We took woolen shirts, heavy socks, rain gear, appropriate footwear and prepared as if we were going camping, which of course we were. We arrived at our launching area the night before and set up base camp in a nearby campground.

Early the next morning, we were packing our duffle bags as the sun broke over the lake. Already we were experiencing the beauty and solitude of the wilderness. There is a primeval atmosphere in this remote area that bespeaks both a peace and an excitement. The children were eager to get started. Unlike ordinary camping when we enjoyed a leisurely breakfast, that morning we had a simple and hurried meal. We put those things we wouldn't need on the trip in the car with a sense of farewell to civilization, for we were going to rough it for 5 or 6 days.

At the outfitters there was a feeling of the old wild west. The canoes were already at the dock for us. The men seemed so casual, in marked contrast to our feeling of anticipation and some bewilderment. Fortunately, I had been on several such trips before, but on those I had shared the labors with other men. Now I felt a heavy, almost ominous, responsibility. What if I should be hurt 2 days out, some 20 or 30 miles from the nearest outpost? Canoes require a man to portage them, I thought. (Later I learned even slightly built women also can handle canoes very ably once they learn how to lift them.) But I put those thoughts aside as we began carefully loading the duffle bags, distributing the weight properly in each canoe.

Soon we had our safety jackets on, and were gingerly getting into the canoes. We began pushing away from the dock. The first thing one notices is how quietly and easily the canoes move along even with considerable weight in them. We experimented with our paddling until we got the maximum force from our strokes and still kept the craft moving straight ahead. Suddenly with all the excitement of launching behind us we noticed the pristine beauty of the sky-blue water and the native pine trees lining the shores.

One of the first requirements is to have a waterproof map of the area readily at hand, with someone assigned as navigator to keep close watch of exactly where one is all the time. Looking across the lake we were not able to identify the location of the passages between lakes. Every tree-lined shore looked continuous. Even the islands blended into this horizon. Unless our navigator pointed precisely the direction we were to go to reach these passages we would have to do a great deal more paddling to find them.

Before long we reached the end of the channel leading from the dock to the large open lake, a distance of over a mile. We found ourselves crossing what appeared to be a huge body of water. The thought occurred to us that we were in a very lightweight craft and our lives depended on its seaworthiness. This is not an uncommon concern the first time out in a canoe. Within a relatively short time, however, we began to have confidence in our canoes, and ourselves, and we began to laugh and sing one of our favorite family songs which we had enjoyed so often while traveling.

By this time it was already mid-morning and the sun was warm. The exertion of paddling soon forced us to begin shedding our jackets and we put on our hats to protect against sunburn. It was a glorious day! The beauty of the area was indescribable. We could hear the incomparable loons calling to each other across the lake. (Later we were to recall that the sound of the loons was one of the thrills of our trip.)

Toward mid-day we asked our navigator to select a campsite where we could stop for lunch. Coincidentally, we would reach our first portage about lunchtime.

Portages are a mixed blessing. They necessitate unloading all the gear and carrying it and the canoes over a primitive path to the next lake. This may be only 100 feet or it may at times be as much as ½ mile or more over rough terrain. After a couple of hours of paddling it always seems a relief to get out on land and walk. But some portages are a challenge and are quite time consuming and tiring. That noon it was a pleasant portage and a beautiful spot to have our trail lunch. After we ate we lay on the bank in the sun and felt a delicious sense of relaxation. We were truly isolated. We could hear only the sounds of nature and the rushing waters of the rapids nearby. Soon the children were off exploring the wilderness and wading in the shallow water of the nearby stream.

With the canoes again loaded we were off on our next lap. Now we were in a new lake. The scenery was different. We noticed that the shores were lined with driftwood, bleached and beautiful on the sand. It was a small lake, only a mile or so across, and the map showed that we could reach the next lake through a navigable channel. The eye couldn't detect the break in the tree-lined shore where the channel was, but the navigator, using the map and a compass, had a bead on its location. Soon we reached the opposite shore and suddenly the channel came into view. It was a relief to know that we were still properly oriented.

Several hours and 2 small portages later we began planning which campsite we would select for the night. We began noticing that several of the camps were already occupied. The thought occurred to us that we might not find a vacant one. With a sense of relief we found that our chosen site was still vacant. It was a beautiful camp on an island, with the tip of the island jutting out into the lake. We pitched camp in a clearing. We had water on both sides of us, with heavy woods to the back of us to protect us from any storm or wind that might come up in the night.

While the children were putting up our tent, I gathered driftwood. Soon we had a blazing campfire. Son Tom already had readied his fishing rod and was heading for a canoe to try his luck at catching a northern pike. The other children had donned their bathing suits and were out in the crystal-clear water, splashing and playing.

Evenings are indescribably spectacular in the lake country. Always I have my camera ready for the sunsets. I must have a dozen or more sunset pictures taken on canoe trips. Each one seems more beautiful than the next. Our favorite evening activity was to hike around to the west side of our island, sit on the rocks and watch the sun slowly disappear in a blaze of glory behind the tree-lined horizon.

Over the years I have learned that it is preferable to set up camp on an island rather than on the mainland. We are much less apt to be bothered by bears. In the times we have followed this practice we have never had bruin visit us in the night. Our daughter, Susan, on the other hand, many years later, was camping with a friend on the mainland. A big she-bear nearly wiped out their food supply for the week on the very first night. Had it not been for fellow canoers sharing their rations, the trip simply would have had to be cut short. Fortunately bears are only after camp food and not the campers themselves. While it is a frightening experience, it isn't often dangerous. However, one doesn't challenge a bear even if she is eating your food right in front of you.

One learns very quickly that, as soon as the sun is down, friendly mosquitoes will welcome you by the thousands. It is then that you appreciate the tight netting in the doorways of your tents. Typically you will need to remain in your tent from dusk onward unless there is a strong breeze playing over your campsite that keeps the mosquitoes back in the trees. Every rose has its thorns, and the thorns for canoers are the insects, especially mosquitoes and what some call "no-see-ums"—small invisible pests that keep your evenings from being too perfect!

A phenomenon you learn your first night out is that sounds carry long distances over water. I recall the first canoe trip I took. We heard the crashing of a tree during the night. It sounded as if it were almost in our campsite. We concluded that a beaver was hard at work. The next morning we searched for the source of the sound and found that the downed tree was a good half mile away.

This night we also were awakened by a noise, one which was frightening in its intensity. There was no mistaking this, however—a thunderstorm was rapidly approaching. Soon the rain was pelting our tent. After the initial apprehension wore off we settled down to sleep, lulled by the pitter-patter of rain on the tent roof several feet above us.

The next morning, as the bright sun broke into our tent, we surveyed the effects of the rain. Fortunately we had a tarpaulin over the table where we had our cooking gear and food. All was intact. Some of the rain did run under the tent, however, and a couple of our sleeping bags were quite damp. We rigged a clothesline and got them in the sun to dry.

It was a beautiful fresh morning, with a slight breeze and a warm sun. We decided we would remain camping there for a day or two, exploring some of the nearby lakes and perhaps doing some fishing. It was a good decision. One lake in particular was a gem. It was relatively small and inaccessible. To reach it we beached our canoe and climbed over rocks and bushes. It was apparent that few people visited this lake. The shores were strewn with great piles of driftwood. We walked along the shore and finally selected a fairly large, unusually shaped piece. Carrying driftwood is like toting an antler—

it doesn't pack very well in a canoe. But we managed and, to this day, it has a place on our patio.

Fishing in canoe country lakes is a fisherman's dream. The pike generally are large and vigorous, providing a real thrill when they are hooked. Fishing is part of the joy of canoeing. It also is a necessity. It is a burden to pack in a week's food supply for 5 people. So we always depend on fish for at least 3 evening meals or more, especially since after the second day our fresh meat has been eaten. This day we were not disappointed. Tom and I chose an area between 2 islands which seemed a likely spot for northern pike to pass. We did not have long to wait. As I was quietly paddling, Tom trolled with a silver minnow, a metal spoon lure. Suddenly his rod bent down to the water and then underneath the canoe. He had hooked a big one! I grabbed the landing net and waited for him to reel in the fish beside the canoe. After several deep dives the northern relented and Tom brought him alongside. For the first time we got a view of him, and he of us apparently. Just as I was dipping the net into the water he dove again, with the brake on the reel buzzing like a rattlesnake. We finally landed him and took him back to show our trophy to the rest of the family. He provided more than a meal for all of us that evening.

After a couple of days we decided to move further along the route, seeking new scenery and adventure. Before long we came to the longest portage of our trip, one almost ½ mile long. Fortunately, the path was through a fairly level and beautiful woods. It took us well over an hour before we were loaded and into the next lake.

The morning of the last day we were greeted with a wind direction and velocity that spelled storm. One quickly learns to read weather signs when out in the woods or on lakes. In fact a wise canoeist will study the elements of weather prediction before embarking on a trip. This day it was obvious that within 12 hours it would be raining. We had camped the night before just after we had made the last portage of the route so we knew we could make good time.

We hadn't fully anticipated the day. As we entered the largest lake on our route we became quite concerned. The wind had increased and the lake had whitecaps on it, a clear sign that waves had built up to a dangerous height. We paddled to the lee side of an island and studied the situation. We had to cross the lake—no question about it—or else change our plans, set up camp, and expect to be rained in for perhaps 2 days.

We decided that the 2 of us most experienced in paddling would take the stern of each canoe. The stern paddler controls the direction and provides the power to move the craft forward. We all donned safety vests, covered our gear, and pushed off. We knew that once we had begun there would be no turning back without the danger of capsizing. We agreed exactly how we would tack across the lake, hitting the waves at just the right angle. It was a thrilling and somewhat frightening experience. In about a half hour we had succeeded in making the crossing. We beached our canoes on the lee side of another island. There we found a grassy, sunny spot and sank to the ground exhausted.

From that point on it was easy going. We arrived at our disembarking dock at mid-afternoon. That evening, after we had traveled by car to a village campground some 40 miles away and had just set up our tent, the weather prediction that we made in the morning was borne out. A major storm had hit the area with rain coming down in sheets. We settled down for a beautiful rest after an adventurous trip, one which we will remember for a lifetime.

EQUIPMENT NEEDED. It is estimated that some 65,000 canoes are sold each year, with sales climbing more than 40 percent annually. A canoe has many characteristics which make its appeal so universal. It is lightweight. One person can lift it, portage it, or put it on top of a car where it can easily be transported. It is inexpensive. It is easily paddled, enabling 2 people to cover upwards of 20 miles in a day without undue exertion. All members of the family can enjoy it, either singly or with others. It glides along smoothly, quietly, and easily, without sound and without the noise of a motor. Canoes require virtually no maintenance, since most are made of aluminum or fiber glass. And since they are portable, they provide the means to explore unspoiled backwaters, inaccessible by motor boats and land vehicles. Canoes are very good for fishing, since they move quietly and do not disturb the fish. For those seeking thrills, canoes can run the white-water rapids of turbulent rivers when under the control of skilled paddlers.

In addition to aluminum and fiber glass, wood, styrene, and polyethylene plastics are used to manufacture canoes. Also, one can still buy wooden frame canoes with canvas or synthetic coverings. Each material has its attributes and proponents.

Canoeing does not require a great outlay in auxiliary equipment. In addition to the canoe, which may cost from $200 up, one needs a yoke to carry it on one's shoulders, 2 paddles, and safety jackets for each person. Beyond this any other purchases will depend on the kind of canoeing activity planned. If you are going on overnight trips you will need camping gear. If you plan to travel, you will need a cartop carrier to haul the canoe. All in all, canoeing does not require a great expense. The equipment requires little or no maintenance and can be used for many years.

It is a possibility that once you become a canoeist you will want to expand your interest to include running rapids, called white-water canoeing. A close cousin to the canoe is the kayak, familiar to most of us as the Eskimo's canoe, which is becoming increasingly popular among sportsmen. No less a personage than Jimmy Carter runs river rapids in canoes and kayaks, which bodes well for the sport. Pope John Paul II reputedly also is a canoeist.

PHYSICAL PREPARATION.   Canoeing is a sport that will provide excellent exercise for the body, especially from the waist up. Portaging, on the other hand, requires good leg muscles and sure footing. For a canoe trip such as those taken in the Boundary Waters Canoe Area, it is likely that you will travel over 50 miles, perhaps as much as 100 miles on a week-long outing. Such trips are especially demanding of the arm and shoulder muscles. It is not advisable to embark on such an undertaking without proper body conditioning.

As mentioned earlier, a canoe trip entails many activities. Swimming, hiking, portaging, and camping, all require some effort. I recall vividly my first exciting canoe trip in the Superior National Forest. The one unpleasant memory of this trip has served me in all successive

Cold water and cold weather canoeing require special precautions. Note that the canoeist is wearing rubberized material for insulation along with his life preserver. He is kneeling near the center of the canoe to ensure stability.

trips. We had paddled over 20 miles that first day. We had at least 5 portages, one of which entailed carrying the canoe, all our gear, and food for the week, up and over a fairly steep rocky path that extended at least ¼ of a mile. Despite refreshing swims after several of the portages, I was exhausted by the time we pitched camp late in the afternoon. I obviously had not been in condition for such exertion and I was paying the price.

WHERE TO GO CANOEING. Every lake, and almost every river, provides the canoeist an opportunity to enjoy this sport. Some rivers are particularly well suited because they are navigable for some distance without impediments of dams, waterfalls, or impassable obstructions of one kind or another.

One of the most beautiful canoeing rivers is the St. Croix, a federally designated Wild River, which forms part of the border between Wisconsin and Minnesota. For some 30 miles, from Taylors Falls to Stillwater, Minnesota, one can leisurely float with the current, observing the beautiful wooded shorelines on either side of the river. There are abundant wildlife, good fishing, and stopping places along the shores or on islands, either for camping or for picnicking. For those wanting to rent canoes there are liveries in Taylors Falls that will help you launch and then arrange to meet you later 30 miles downstream and bring you back.

Many states have similar areas. State tourist, conservation, or natural resource departments can usually provide information on canoeing opportunities. They also provide directories of camping facilities along the routes. The American Canoe Association has information on canoeing routes and outfitters, as well as other helpful material. Its official magazine, *Canoe*, provides a source of useful suggestions for both the experienced and the beginning canoeist. Among the better guides describing various canoer's waterways, scenery, and camping spots is Robert Colwell's *Introduction to Water Trails in America*, listed at the end of this chapter.

The acknowledged best canoeing routes in the world are in the Quetico–Superior forest area. They have become so renowned that one has to have a reservation to enter the area. In this way the number of canoers can be limited to the number of camping facilities available. Superior has 1200 miles of canoe routes and most of them are well mapped and have campsites with sturdy tables and fireplaces, and even latrines. Despite this seeming over-civilizing of the wilderness area, the campsites are fairly unobtrusive. The water is still potable. Because of the increasingly stringent regulations on use of this area, it is well to find out the latest restrictions before leaving home. The use of open fires in wilderness areas, for example, is forbidden if there has not been adequate rainfall. Also, use of cans and bottles is forbidden to avoid litter problems.

TIPS FOR OLDER CANOERS.   Canoeing requires the use of a number of muscles. In preparation for any canoe outing it is wise to assess one's physical ability to undertake the activity. A simple Saturday or Sunday afternoon outing is not very demanding, of course, but if one is planning a week-long canoe trip in the wilderness, it is quite another matter. Preparations for the trip should include physical conditioning, as well as food, shelter, and clothing requirements. On a wilderness trip you may be required to lift an 85 to 90 pound canoe onto your shoulders and off again, several times a day, depending upon how many portages you have en route. You have to carry the canoe by yourself (which works better than carrying it with someone) for varying distances even as long as a half mile, sometimes over rocky, uneven, or perhaps hilly terrain, occasionally working your way around and under trees. In addition to the canoe you will have to carry the food and gear, such as fishing rods and tackle, tent, tarpaulin, sleeping bags, air mattresses, cooking utensils, clothes, and canoe paddles. To do this requires considerable physical exertion. Therefore, if there is any doubt in your mind as to whether you can hack it, you should have a frank conversation with your physician before departing.

Safety should be a part of the planning for any canoe trip. Personal flotation devices not only are a legal requirement but make very good sense. The canoe outfitter can provide these if you do not own your own. How to get in and out of a canoe is something you should learn before you start on your outing. An accidental dunking, of you or your equipment, is not the way to start a canoe trip. Should you get caught in a squall, keep low in the canoe to prevent capsizing. Should you capsize, by all means stay with the canoe. It will float and support you as well, even if it may be partially submerged.

Don't start out on a canoe trip without a thorough review of all your needs, or probable needs, for the trip. Any good book on canoeing will provide you with a checklist against which you can determine your requirements. Be prepared for some rain, and the ensuing dampness in camp. Proper shoes are particularly important in this regard. Well-oiled, heavy-soled hiking boots are very good for portages, to prevent foot bruises from rocks on the trail. Once in camp, a pair of sneakers can be very comfortable and also, because of their rubber construction, can resist dampness.

It is important to remember that on a canoe trip you may be several days away from any assistance should you become ill or injure yourself. A well-planned first-aid kit is an essential item for you to take along. This is especially important for older people whose requirements for medical aid may be more acute than those of a younger person.

If you are new to canoeing, it can be very helpful to learn some fundamentals about the sport before you set out on your own. For example, there is a definite technique one must learn to be able to lift the canoe on to one's shoulders by oneself. It isn't difficult once learned and anyone can do it. Knowing how to manage a swamped canoe also can be a matter of survival if you should upset back in the wilderness canoe country, away from help. One should learn the basics of canoe paddling and canoe handling in such difficult situations as strong winds or high waves. Knowing how to load a canoe, and what the load capacities of canoes are, is essential for long canoe trips. How to manage adverse weather, such as heavy rain, to protect not only yourself but your gear, is also good information. There are techniques to be learned on how to pack your equipment, food, supplies, and clothing so that they won't be lost in the event of a capsize. Also it is extremely helpful to pack your personal belongings,

food, and utensils in the right order so that the first thing you need isn't at the bottom of the duffle bag or pack sack. Where does one go to get such instruction? The Grumman Boat Company has compiled a useful directory, listed at the end of the chapter, of places to go to learn about canoeing. YMCA's often provide such help. Also check with your local sporting goods stores and canoe outfitters for advice on where to go.

Choosing the right time of the summer to go on your canoe trip may make an important difference in your success and enjoyment of the venture. This may vary somewhat, depending upon the part of the country you are in. Try to avoid the rainy season, or the hot and humid season, if possible. Dampness makes camping unpleasant and also encourages mosquitoes to breed, adding to the unpleasantness. In the Boundary Waters Canoe Area I have found that late August is almost consistently the best time of the year. The area is less crowded, since families with children have completed their vacations. The fall colors are beginning to show. The air is a bit crisper. The water has cleared from summer algae. The fish are biting better again. And the weather is likely to be better at that time of the summer. If possible, try to pick a week during which you will have a full moon. It adds one more attraction to your trip. Sitting around a campfire, beside a lake in the canoe country, with a full moon shimmering across the water, is just about the perfect setting for relaxation and enjoyment. Can you think of any better one?

FOR MORE INFORMATION

Because of the increasing popularity of canoeing there are numerous books available to assist beginners as well as the more experienced to plan canoe trips. Bookstores, libraries, and many sporting goods stores have books and other literature available. Above all do your homework before you go. Canoeing can be a great experience or a disaster, depending in large part on adequate preparation. Preparation, in fact, is part of the fun of it. Planned right, a canoe trip will be one of the most enjoyable and memorable experiences of your life.

Books:

Angier, Bradford, and Zack Taylor. *Introduction to Canoeing.* Harrisburg, Pa., Stackpole, 1973. $3.95.
> A good beginner's guide. Illustrated with drawings. Simply explains equipment, canoe designs, where to canoe, how, what to take.

Bolz, J. Arnold. *Portage into the Past: By Canoe Along the Minnesota–Ontario Boundary Waters.* Minneapolis, University of Minnesota Press, 1960. $6.50.
> An account of the canoe trip taken by the author following the route of the voyageurs some 250 years earlier. Numerous references are given to the historical accounts of the early voyages of the traders and explorers. Delightfully illustrated by the noted wildlife artist, Francis Lee Jaques.

Colwell, Robert. *Introduction to Water Trails in America.* Harrisburg, Pa., Stackpole, 1973. $3.95.
> A detailed guide to America's numerous canoeing waterways, describing the scenery and camping places.

Duncanson, Michael E. *A Paddler's Guide to the Boundary Waters Canoe Area.* Virginia, Minn., W. A. Fisher, 1976. $4.95.
> Provides detailed maps and descriptions of 31 wilderness canoe routes in the Superior National Forest of northern Minnesota.

McPhee, John. *The Survival of the Bark Canoe.* New York, Farrar, Straus and Giroux, 1975. $7.95.

Michaelson, Mike, and Keith Ray. *Canoeing.* Chicago, Regnery, 1975. $4.95.
> Well-illustrated guide for the beginning canoeist. Describes canoe designs, paddling technique, camping, and 10 favorite canoe trips.

Olson, Sigurd. *Listening Point.* New York, Knopf, 1958.
———. *The Singing Wilderness.* New York, Knopf, 1956.
> The series of books by Sigurd Olson provides delightful reading and a flavor of canoeing in the wilderness. The author is a noted naturalist with the gift of expression that reveals the intimacy he feels for the canoe country. The titles above are of special interest to the canoeist.

Magazines:

Canoe. Bi-monthly. Voyager Publications Inc., 131 E. Murray St., Fort Wayne, Ind. 46803. $6.00 per year, or with membership in American Canoe Association, 4620 East Evans Avenue, Denver, Co. 80222. Membership $6.00 per year.
> Covers canoeing, kayaking, and white-water running. Useful for information on where to canoe, equipment, personalities, and organizations. Keeps you up to date on developments.

River World. 9 times a year, February through October. World Publications, Box 366, Mountain View, Ca. 94043. $8.00 per year.

Covers canoeing and river running, as well as kayaking and rubber rafting. Special features on racing, equipment, conditioning, and national developments.

Wilderness Camping. Bi-monthly. Fitzgerald Communications, Inc., 1597 Lemon Street, Schenectady, N.Y. 12309. $6.95 per year.

Directories:

One manufacturer of canoes, Grumman Boats, has compiled several directories, listed below, which are most useful, and free. They can be obtained by writing for them at Marathon, N.Y. 13803.

Rent-A-Canoe Directory

Arranged by states, this listing of over 900 liveries in 46 states is one of the best guides available. It is ample evidence of the popularity of canoes and the extensive opportunities that exist for canoeing. It also includes a list of books and magazines on canoeing, many of which are guides published by agencies of various states. A most useful directory.

Learn-To-Canoe Directory

This is a listing of clubs and other organizations, by states, where one can obtain instruction in canoe handling and safety.

The Grumman Book Rack for Canoeists

An interesting compilation of books currently available about canoeing. Each entry is briefly described and provides prices and publishers' addresses where the books can be purchased.

12 *Sailing*

'T IS THE SET of the sails, and not the gales, which tells us the way to go" was a line in a poem I learned as a youngster, and I think of it every time I go sailing. "How in the world can you sail against the wind?" That is often the question posed as I take guests sailing for their first time. It certainly is one of the mysteries of wind power. My explanation leaves them still somewhat puzzled and largely unconvinced. Fascinating as this phenomenon is, it is only one of the many reasons people enjoy sailing.

I was reared in a land-locked area where a creek was my only exposure to water. Sailing was something I knew only from books, and I imagined it was limited to the rich. Being a farm boy from a relatively low-income family, I never dared aspire to enjoy sailing, much less own a boat. Therefore, when many years later I acquired a lake cabin, among my first water equipment was an Alcort "Sailfish." It was especially suitable for the children because of its light weight, easy maneuvering, simple rigging, and low cost. It was less satisfactory for adults but still it was great fun; and it was the beginning of many years of enjoyment of the fascinating sport of sailing.

To fully appreciate sailing, one has to do it. First-timers are always a bit frightened. Coupled with the excitement of quietly gliding over the surface of the water, propelled by the force of the wind on the beautiful sail above you, is one's apprehension as the boat tips and leans. Surely, you think, it is going to capsize. For that reason I equip each guest with a life jacket to allay fears of going overboard and panicking in the water. Tipping over with a sailboat, while possible, and not infrequent in sailing regattas where maximum speed in strong winds is the objective, is not a very common event in pleasure sailing. But even if it does occur, normal precautions and proper handling of the craft can right it and no one is the worse off except for getting wet.

I am a cautious sailor and avoid going out if there is a gusty wind. I, too, become apprehensive when the boat tips. My eye is constantly turned to the sky to watch for wind clouds and sudden storms. I thus am not taken by surprise by weather conditions. If anything, I err on the side of being becalmed occasionally. Embarrassing as that may be, the situation can be parlayed into a laughing matter.

The Alcort "Sailfish," the first of my two sailboats, is a unique craft. It is a glorified surfboard with a sail. It is fast, maneuverable, versatile, and suitable for only 1 adult or 2 youngsters. One sails the "Sailfish" wearing a swimming suit, for an unexpected gust of wind, or perhaps mishandling of the sail or rudder, will tip it over and throw the occupants in the water. This does not come as a surprise, of course, and you are fully prepared to cope with the situation. In a minute the boat can be righted, you climb on board and away you go. My youngsters spent as much time in the water as on board, it seemed, and this was part of their fun. My daughter, now an adult, still prefers the "Sailfish" to my larger boat.

A good beginner's boat is the 14-foot single-masted sloop. It has a mainsail and a jib. The jib complicates sailing only slightly but aids considerably in getting the most power from the wind. It is a beautiful sight to see this sailboat with full sails, as one tacks back and forth across the lake. On small lakes one frequently has to change course, reset the sail, adjust the jib, and shift the weight of the guests in the boat. It is a continuous activity, especially on tree-lined lakes with inlets and bays, for the wind currents are constantly shifting. On larger lakes one can secure the lines, set the sail and course, and sit back and enjoy the breeze and the ride.

One experiences a joyful contentment mixed with excitement while sailing. Imagine a warm, sunny day with a refreshing breeze—conditions to enjoy many outdoor activities. Such a day is especially pleasant for sailing. The only sounds are the fluttering of the sail, the swishing of water at the bow, and your own conversation. When the conditions are just right you feel the surge of wind power and the shuddering of the boat as it sweeps forward. You keep adjusting the set of the sail and the rudder to the leaning of the boat to achieve the maximum speed. It is then that you are fascinated with the mysteries that send you over the water at a speed that seems faster than the wind that propels you. This is the great mystery about sailing. It is especially noticeable with iceboating. An iceboat is essentially a sled with a sail. A moderate breeze can propel the craft 50 mph or more, as much as 2½ times faster than the wind.

TYPES OF SMALL SAILBOATS.   Sailboats have a wide range in size. There are the small "Sailfish" or "Sunfish" models sometimes called sailing boards. These are about 10 feet long, made of wood or fiber glass. They are actually quite portable and can be carried by 2 people, placed on top of your car, and launched in any suitable lake.

A typical family-type sailboat is the sloop, about 14–16 feet long, made of wood or fiber glass, and easily transportable on a trailer. Usually, because of the high mast, such boats are left in the water and moored a short distance offshore. They have a centerboard rather than a heavy keel and have a mainsail, and occasionally a jib. They can carry 3 or 4 adults and are suitable for small inland lakes.

For large lakes that may have fairly big waves and perhaps an occasional strong wind, larger sailboats are made having heavy keels weighing one or more tons. These serve to stabilize the boats and keep them from capsizing. In addition to the mainsail such craft will have a jib and often a spinnaker—a large sail that balloons out in front

of the boat, pulling it along with additional force and speed. Because such boats will venture out from shore some distance, they usually have auxiliary motor power to bring them in in case of adverse weather conditions. Some boats have sleeping and eating facilities and can be used for overnight stays aboard.

Beyond this are the sea-going craft that may have a complex sail system, living facilities, a large inboard motor, and large decks. These may be as long as 40 feet or more, with keels weighing several tons. Such boats, once they are transported to their home body of water, generally are kept there and merely dry-docked over the winter. These boats can sail the Great Lakes or some oceans, and excursions may last for days.

Chances are that if you haven't sailed by now you may not aspire to the large, seagoing cruisers and yachts. The family-type sloop is a very good size for one's introduction to sailing. It is relatively low cost, transportable, easily maintained, can be learned quickly, and is very enjoyable. One of the memorable sights we happened upon during a trip to Europe was on a late afternoon in Holland. We were driving north of Amsterdam and came upon a delightful small village. Just as we were approaching the canal at the edge of the village, we were stopped as the bridge was raised. Soon 4 or 5 small sailboats,

Rigging up a sailboat.

sloop-size, silently eased through the canal in front of us and out into the larger canal. It was a beautiful, envious moment, and one I often think about as I rig my own sailboat.

With special rigging, a canoe can be converted to a sailboat. Since canoes have no keels or centerboards, they are equipped with a double centerboard, called "lee boards," that drops down on both sides of the canoe. In some instances outriggers are attached to make the canoe more stable. This system has the advantage of increasing the use of the canoe and reducing the total cost of water equipment.

An increasingly popular sailboat is the catamaran. It basically consists of a bridge or platform, sometimes of canvas, between 2 pontoons that have been fastened 4 or 5 feet apart by a welded structure. Catamarans are transportable, relatively lightweight, and quite stable. They are not especially comfortable, however, for one has to lie down on the platform while sailing. Older adults, I have found, prefer to sit down in a reasonably comfortable position to get the most enjoyment from sailing.

Sailboats may require an expenditure of upwards of $1000 for a sloop of fairly simple design. More elaborate boats, racing craft, or finely finished wood-decked boats, of course, cost more. One must remember that a sailboat will in all likelihood be moored out in the water throughout the entire summer. Maintenance, therefore, can be a major chore unless durable materials and finishes are used. This is one of the reasons for the popularity of fiber glass boats which require very little maintenance. Sailcloth is often an artificial fabric, dacron, that can withstand sun and moisture, and will retain its strength against the force of the wind, and the fluttering and sometimes whipping action it undergoes.

LEARNING TO SAIL.   If you get into sailing, you are exposed to a whole new vocabulary of sailing terms. To appear erudite you may want to have some of these in mind to impress your friends. It won't make you a better sailor—unless, of course, you have a crew with whom you communicate. In such cases it is well to all speak the same jargon, especially in regattas, where every move may make the difference between losing and winning. As a beginner it might be advisable, although it is certainly not necessary, to attend a course on sailing. If, on the other hand, you intend to take up sailing seriously, want to join a yacht club, keep your boat in crowded mooring areas, and converse with other sailors, it no doubt will take more than reading a book to educate you in the art of sailing. Sailing instruction often is available through the adult education programs of your local school system, through yacht clubs, or the U.S. Coast Guard auxiliary. Lists of schools and courses can often be obtained from sailboat dealers and yacht clubs.

The sailor easily handles the tiller and line controlling the sail, while his weight is properly distributed to provide ballast to the boat.

TIPS FOR OLDER SAILORS. Sailing entails so few hazards, and so little by way of heavy exertion or endurance, that it is one of the ideal sports activities for older people. Naturally one is limited to areas where there are adequate lakes or rivers, but this would include almost every state, and many places within most states. Unless one has a regular mooring place to keep the craft all summer, one is limited also to small, relatively portable boats that can be trailered. Most sloop-size boats are not at all heavy, so loading and unloading at public landings or docks again is a simple procedure.

For older people the small sailing boards that can be carried on top of the car are not very comfortable and, in my opinion, are generally unsuitable unless one is a good swimmer, fairly agile, and likes to sail alone. A boat that is a minimum of 14 feet long is still a small boat and can easily be handled, and in such a craft one can sit fairly comfortably and can be joined by a couple of friends or one's spouse. I have often seen such boats traveling along highways with the same facility as other trailered boats.

If you have woodworking or shop activity as a hobby you may want to look into the possibility of making your own boat. One can buy plans for different sized boats, or kits that require assembling. Build it in your garage, not your basement!

Sailing usually will be enjoyed on sunny days, I suspect. Since a sailing outing is likely to last for some time, perhaps as much as a half day or even more, the occupants will be exposed to a great deal of sun, both directly and reflected from the water. It is very easy to become overexposed on such days, whether the sun is shining brightly or the sky is partly overcast. Adequate precautions must be taken to prevent painful sunburn. A sailing hat, use of blocking cream or suntan lotion, and thin wraps to protect the body from the sun, are advisable. Dark glasses are essential also. A word of caution with respect to glasses and sunglasses. One is subject to sudden gusts while out on the water. I have seen glasses blown off people and into the water. Since that makes for a costly outing, precautions are in order.

While it is generally advisable to wear flotation vests when in any water craft, it is particularly recommended while sailing. The sailboat is subject to lateral wind pressures. At times in gusty weather one cannot always predict when an unusually strong gust may hit the sail. Unless the person at the tiller and in control of the mainsail is alert, it is possible for the boat to suddenly tip or even capsize. In that unlikely event, life jackets become extremely important to protect the occupants from panic, or to help keep them afloat should they be accidentally hurt while being thrown into the water. In any case, having a life vest on gives one a feeling of security and contributes to the enjoyment of sailing.

A friend of ours, Carl Jackson, recently completed a 51-day solo sail from Maine to Ireland. He did it in a 30-foot craft. In his mid-50's, he had fulfilled a lifelong dream of crossing the Atlantic Ocean in his own sailboat. The accounts of his voyage make fascinating reading. Few people aspire to such adventure, but it does illustrate that even the rigors of such a voyage can be withstood by older people, and that the world of adventure is open to us regardless of age. Reading about Carl Jackson's trip I was reminded of a conversation he and I had many years ago. It was near midnight and we were crossing big Rainy Lake at the Minnesota–Canada border, in a small 16-foot aluminum boat. The wind was blowing and it was raining hard. We were making our way across the lake, dead reckoning as we went, heading for an island where our wives were waiting for us in his small cabin. To say I was apprehensive is to put it mildly. Carl was thriving on the excitement and danger of the trip, relying on his familiarity with the lake and its various rocky shoals and outcroppings to get us home safely. Our discussion that perilous night has made my own life richer and fuller. Carl persuaded me that such challenges as we were then experiencing provided the leavening by which living was changed from a humdrum existence to one of adventure and excitement. Danger, he felt, is the important ingredient against which we must pit our wits. It isn't something to avoid as much as it is to challenge. The process is invigorating. While it is foolhardy to take unnecessary chances, to continuously "play it safe" can be terribly dull. I am certain that my experience that night, riding the waves of a rough and threatening lake, had an influence in my decision to take up skiing at 55 years of age, buy a motorcycle at 60, and, although unsuccessful because of lack of wind currents, attempt to arrange a ride in a sailplane in Switzerland among the Alps last year.

FOR MORE INFORMATION

If your interest in sailing has been aroused, why not induce a friend with a boat to take you for an outing, so you can feel the experience? Perhaps you won't like it, but I doubt it. More likely you will want to read more about it. The following books and magazines will give you some idea of the literature available for people like yourself. Check with your local public library or bookstore for these or other titles they may have.

Article:
Graham, Robin Lee. "A Teen-Ager Sails the World Alone," *National Geographic*, October, 1968, pp. 445–491.
Books:
Creagh-Osborne, Richard. *Dinghy Building.* 2nd Ed. Tuckahoe, N.Y., De Graff, 1977. $15.00.
D'Alpugert, Lon. *Successful Sailing.* New York, Macmillan, 1973. $1.95.
Drummond, A. H., Jr. *The Complete Beginner's Guide to Sailing.* New Ed. New York, Doubleday, 1975. $5.95.

Editors of *Rudder. Good Sailing: An Illustrated Course on Sailing.* New York, McKay, 1975. $8.95.

Farnham, Moulton H. *Sailing for Beginners.* New York, Macmillan, 1975. $5.95.

Geen, Fox. *A Handbook of Small Boat Cruising.* New York, Quadrangle, 1974. $7.95.

George, M. B. *Basic Sailing.* New York, Hearst Books, 1971. $2.95.

Gibbs, Tony. *Practical Sailing.* New York, Hearst Books, 1971. $3.95.

Hart, John. *Modern Small Boat Sailing.* New York, Transatlantic, 1974. $15.00.

Heaton, Peter. *Sailing.* New York, Penguin. $2.95.

Law, Donald. *Beginner's Guide to Sailing.* New York, Drake, 1974. $4.95.

Mitchell, Leeds, Jr. *Introduction to Sailing.* Harrisburg, Pa., Stackpole, 1974. $3.95.

Moore, James, and Alan Turvey. *Starting Sailing.* New York, Doubleday, 1974. $5.95.

Muhlhausen, John. *Wind & Sail: A Primer for Beginning Sailors.* New York, Quadrangle, 1971. $7.95.

Robinson, B. *America's Sailing Book.* New York, Scribners, 1976. $12.95.

Smith, Rufus G. *Sailing Made Easy.* New York, Dodd Mead, 1974. $5.00.

Stevenson, Peter. *Sailboats You Can Build.* Radnor, Pa., Chilton, 1977. $5.95.

Magazines:

Motor Boating & Sailing. Monthly. 959 Eighth Avenue, New York 10019. $10.00 per year.

Sail. Monthly. 38 Commercial Wharf, Boston, Mass. 02110. $12 per year.

Sailing. Monthly. 125 East Main Street, Port Washington, Wi. 53074. $9.50 per year.

Sea. Monthly. 1515 Broadway, New York 10036. $8.50 per year.

Skipper. Monthly. 2nd Street at Spa Creek, Annapolis, Md. 21404. $8.00 per year.

Yachting: Power and Sail. Monthly. 50 West 44th Street, New York 10036. $12.00 per year.

13   *Bicycling*

A RAILROAD crossing in Holland, some 15 years ago, was the setting for a most unusual sight. An approaching train set the warning bell clanging. Soon the long gate gently lowered to block the flow of traffic across the track. In the few minutes that it took for the train to pass there assembled a dozen or so waiting automobiles. But what was astonishing were the hundreds of bicyclists who also gathered in that brief period. As the gate lifted the mass movement of those cyclists was a phenomenon I have not as yet seen in the United States.

Gradually, like the Europeans, we Americans are taking to riding bicycles. Some estimate there are as many as 100 million of us, giving rise to the claim that bicycling is the top outdoor activity in the United States today.

Although some progress is evident in the recognition of this tremendous interest in bicycling, there is still much to be done if we are to provide facilities similar to those available in Europe that will give bikers the paths necessary for safe and enjoyable bicycling. Too often cyclists must compete with automobiles on city streets and highways. Too often they are scorned, treated with disdain, or worse, ignored by the motorist.

Some progress is evident, here and there, however. New bikeways occasionally are created from abandoned railroad tracks. In Ohio, for example, the former Penn Central tracks between Akron and Cleveland provide a 30-mile bike path. Wisconsin now has upwards of 100 miles of bike paths, using old rail beds. Many city parks now provide bike as well as pedestrian pathways. Some cities close picturesque streets to auto traffic on Sundays, reserving them for bikers, walkers, and joggers. Lake and river shores increasingly have such paths. In New York, along the Mohawk River, hiking and biking paths have been developed. But until we greatly improve the lot of the bicyclists in this country, there will still be many people who fear accidents and thus will be deterred from taking up bicycling as a form of transportation as well as a means of exercising and a source of enjoyment. After all, safety is no accident.

I cannot help but admire an elderly lady I often see in the little Wisconsin town near our lake cottage. Daily she rides her 3-wheeled bike around the park or into town for her shopping. It is a practical solution to her transportation problem in a community that has no public transportation facilities. Recently we visited Germany and there we saw another solution to this need—the mo-ped. These modified bicycles carry a small motor. They are ubiquitous, used by young and old alike. Still prevalent in Germany are the simple "balloon-tired" bicycles, most of which appear to have been used for many years. It was especially interesting to see many, many older women using their bikes for shopping or general transportation. There is one big difference in Europe—the drivers respect the bicyclists! Here we threaten them, partly I think because bikers are forced to use the automobile's "right-of-way."

For more than a hundred years, half the time since the invention of the bicycle, Americans have enjoyed bicycling. Apparently the sport reached its peak of popularity about the turn of the century. Only in recent years has that popularity been revived. Today bicycling again is rapidly growing in popularity among riders of all ages. Energy-conscious college youth, particularly, have taken to the bicycle as a means of transportation, as can be witnessed on any campus. Many adults and older people also see in bicycle riding a combination of enjoyment and fitness. Along with swimming and jogging, bicycling is one of the best means of exercising. It is, of course, especially good for conditioning the legs, but it also improves the heart and circulatory system. For these reasons the stationary bicycle, or bicycle ergometer, has been developed to provide an indoor means of maintaining fitness through cycling. Adjustments on the exerciser can increase or decrease resistance to pedaling, thus simulating varying bicycling conditions and adapting the exercise to the level desired.

The resurgence of interest in bicycling is a phenomenon of the 70's. Today more bicycles are sold than automobiles. More of them are sold to people over 18 than under, signifying that the bicycle no longer is regarded only as a toy for children. It is not uncommon for all members of a family to have their own bicycles.

A young friend of mine recently described, in ecstatic terms, his experience in bicycle touring. His longest outing was from St. Paul, Minnesota, to Sun Valley, Idaho. At first one would be inclined to observe that this is okay for youngsters but not for anyone past 50. Wrong! A recent issue of *Modern Maturity* describes the various adventures of a 60-year old grandmother, K. C. Arnett. Her current activity is riding her bike across America. While that may be a bit ambitious, bicycle touring for older adults is becoming more common. An increasingly familiar sight on highways are the cars with bicycles on top or on the bumpers. Chances are these folk are heading for a bicycle tour, or returning from one.

Where to go touring is a matter of personal choice. It can be Anyplace, U.S.A. or Canada. The availability of youth hostels—places to stay at very reasonable rates—is an important consideration. The eastern states and Canada offer good hostels and motels, as well as colonial history, beautiful scenery, and varying coastlines. Other parts of the country have their own attractive features. The *North American Bicycle Atlas* published by the American Youth Hostels, Inc., Delaplane, Virginia 22025, is a good place to begin planning your bicycle tour. Other touring books also will provide hints on equipment, clothing, choice of bike, and other necessary information.

Bicycle camping provides the complete outdoor experience. Unlike bicycle touring, which relies on sleeping accommodations and food found at overnight stops, bicycle camping is a totally self-reliant activity. Like backpacking, bike camping can lead you to out-of-the-way, beautiful places not visited by the ordinary bicyclist or tourist. It requires extreme care in selection of your equipment and pack to keep weight at a minimum, generally to no more than 50 pounds. Your tent, sleeping bag, cooking utensils, and food, as well as your clothing must be chosen with weight, comfort, and enjoyment in mind. You should be in condition and have previous camping experience before venturing on a bicycle camping tour. Even then, following the advice and directions in a good camping book is important to avoid making mistakes that may mar the enjoyment of the trip.

There are bicycles designed for different purposes. A review of available models will show excellent vehicles made by both American and foreign manufacturers. Until recently, American manufacturers concentrated on the children's market, leaving foreign manufacturers to provide vehicles for adult and professional bicyclists. Some 300 brands of imported bicycles are believed to be available in the U.S. Gradually, American manufacturers are successfully competing in the adult market, in which some 12 million bicycles are sold each year. The potential buyer has such an array of equipment and models available that advice from a reliable dealer or knowledgeable friend is essential in getting the best bicycle for the purpose.

Costs of bicycles will depend on many factors. The average bicyclist should expect to pay a minimum of $100 for a 10-speed bike, the popular model used by many people today. Racing and special purpose bikes may cost $500 or more.

Once you become a biker you will soon learn of others with the same interest. Often, in the best American tradition, out of such relationships a club is formed. Consequently, today there are clubs in most populated areas. The Bicycle Institute of America has attempted to develop a directory of established clubs, some of which are under the sponsorship of various groups—business, religious, senior citizens, employee groups, etc. The Sierra Club, among its various special interest groups, has many bike clubs around the country. The League of American Wheelmen, 19 South Bothwell, Palatine, Illinois 60067, can provide information on existing clubs or how to start one. Club membership will assure you the enjoyment of sharing outings, activities, information, and bicycling events. Rand McNally's *All About Bicycling* contains a 14-page directory of clubs, some with interesting names: Friends of Bikecology (Santa Barbara); Redwood Velocipedes; Pedal Pushers (Sun City); Wheelmen of the Past Century; Long Beach Sprockets; Pedali Alpini; Orangevale Sidewinders; and Valley Spokesman. As a hint to its objective, one such organization is named Hip Trimmers Bicycle Club (Naples, Florida).

An example of forthright honesty is the Huff & Puff Bicycle Club. Finally, as if to provide a fitting emphasis to this chapter, the club in Lakewood, Colorado, is called Bicycles Now! You don't, of course, need a club, nor do you necessarily have to go touring or camping. Just get a bicycle and start riding. That will be experience enough to stimulate your interest.

TIPS FOR OLDER BIKERS. It is likely that everyone, at one time or another, has tried riding a bicycle. Once having learned it, one is not likely to have forgotten the technique. The bicycle is a simple machine that more and more older people are using for gentle exercise. Mainly it exercises the legs, but long rides will also require some endurance. You might as well start out easy for the first several

times. Even then you probably will experience some muscle strain. Stick to safe areas until you build up your confidence and sure balance. An easy ride around the park rather than on streets should be an enjoyable re-introduction to bicycling.

Many of the multi-speed bicycles are designed to place the rider in what appears to be a racing posture. Seats are high, handle bars curve downward and under. Such designs place us older people in what seems to me a fairly awkward position. Frankly, I don't find such a posture comfortable. Some authors advocate for older people the more traditional bicycle, which allows a fairly upright sitting position. Rather than trying to conform to the current trend, you may enjoy your biking experience more if you adjust your bicycle seat and handlebars to more "normal" positions.

One should remember that bicycling can be a social venture, unlike some other sports. Two can ride along side by side, converse, and enjoy the scenery, much the same as in walking, with the added advantage of covering more territory. Walking requires that each individual select the gait most comfortable for himself, and this varies one to another. Two people on bicycles, on the other hand, can adjust their pace to each other quite easily. It is not uncommon to see a mother, father, and small children all riding as a group, with no apparent strain on any of them. There really is no reason why grandma and grandpa can't join the group and not require any special considerations.

It isn't difficult to identify any number of quite old people who bike. Mal Wickham, 91-year-old student at the University of Wisconsin, rides his bike regularly, as well as jogs. Dr. Paul Dudley White rode a bicycle until his death at 87. He ascribed a number of health benefits to bicycling. The President's Council on Physical Fitness advocates regular biking, as well as other exercise, as a means of getting and staying fit. To stimulate interest in such activities the Council has set up a personal achievement award, with a set of requirements which include riding a minimum of 650 miles in 4 months, with a limit of no more than 13 miles per day. This is to assure regular daily activity rather than an accumulation of credits in a few long trips.

Despite the fact that biking is an appropriate and fun activity for older people, one should not embark on a long bike outing without making certain that such a trip does not require exertion beyond one's capacity. This will vary with each individual and can best be determined by a doctor.

One should also note that bicycle riding, particularly on city streets, is not without its safety hazards. It appears from the statistics that older riders are far more prone to serious accidents than are young children under 14. There are safety guidelines for bicycling and one's self-interest is served by learning and following these. Selecting the right bike will go a long way to increasing your safety.

Your own precautions and carefulness are also important. Keeping your machine in top working order helps, especially proper adjustment of brakes, inflation of tires, oiling of drive chain, and working of the shift mechanism. One important precaution that everyone should take if riding a bicycle after dark is to wear reflectors on his pant legs, on the wheels of the bike, across his shoulders, and on the rear and front of the bicycle. A fully reflectorized biker in front of the headlights of an oncoming car is a dramatic sight and certain to lead the driver to be cautious. Keeping your pant legs from becoming caught in the chain sprocket will prevent one of the most common causes of accidents. If you intend to ride your bike on city streets it is useful to have a bright flag or banner attached to the rear of your bike by a long flexible lightweight staff. This waves easily and alerts motorists to your presence.

Some older people, and younger ones too, have found additional security in wearing a lightweight helmet. Many bike falls result in head injuries, which might be prevented with helmet protection. Also, bright-colored clothing and helmets are added eye-catching devices to call motorists' attention to your presence.

In general, bike riding for older people is not much different than for younger folk. Older riders are more concerned about their personal safety, and recognize that the consequences of a fall or accident are generally more serious for them than for younger bicyclists. Basically what is required is normal cautious riding, and once one adopts reasonable care there is no reason why bicycling shouldn't be one of the most enjoyable of activities.

FOR MORE INFORMATION

Books on bicycling abound, and they are easily available from your bookstore or local public library. Magazines for bikers also can be consulted at the library and once you become acquainted with a favorite title, you may want to subscribe on your own. Below are listed a few typical books and magazines you may want to look at. Others also undoubtedly will be accessible to you at the library. Have fun reading, riding, and . . . !

Books:

Alth, Max. *All About Bikes and Bicycling.* New York, Berkley, 1976. $1.50.
  Simple advice for the beginner and helpful hints for the biker with experience. Will also serve as a manual for maintenance and repair of your bike. A good book to carry with you on your bicycling outing.
All About Bicycling. Chicago, Rand McNally. $4.95.
  Chock full of information on bicycling, including American and foreign model bicycles, bicycle touring and camping, clubs, history, and bicycling and health. Well illustrated.

Belt, Forest, and Bonnie C. Smith. *Easi-Guide to Multispeed Bicycling.* Indianapolis, Ind., Howard W. Sams, 1974. $3.50.

Copiously illustrated. A good beginner's guide.

The Bicycle Driver's Guide. Seattle, Wash., Outdoor Empire Pub., 1973.

A practical pamphlet, aimed at youth but equally applicable to adults. Prepared by the Washington State Superintendent of Public Instruction and the Washington State Patrol.

Fichter, George S., and Keith Kingbay. *Bicycling.* Racine, Wi., Western Publishing, 1974. $2.95.

Fully illustrated. Informative for the beginner and interesting reading for the experienced.

Kingbay, Keith. *Inside Bicycling.* Chicago, Regnery, 1976. $4.95.

Written by an expert, this is a helpful handbook on all aspects of bicycling.

Sloane, Eugene A. *The New Complete Book of Bicycling.* New York, Simon & Schuster, 1974. $12.50.

Magazines:

American Bicyclist & Motorcyclist. Monthly. Cycling Press, Inc., 461 8th Ave., New York 10001. $10 per year.

Bicycle Spokesman. Bi-monthly. Hub Publishing Co., 119 East Palatine Rd., Suite 109, Palatine, Ill. 60067. $8.00 per year.

Bicycling. Monthly. Capital Management Publications, 33 East Minor St., Emmaus, Pa. 18049. $12.00 per year.

Bike World. Monthly. World Publications, Box 366, Mountain View, Ca. 94040. $8.50 per year.

The League of American Wheelmen Bulletin. The League, 19 South Bothwell, Palatine, Ill. 60067. With membership, $8.00 per year.

T ENNIS, in the minds of some, may be thought of as a game for the young. The fact is that it is a noble game for those over 50. We began playing when we were about 60 and it has been an absorbing sport. Now during the summer we play several times a week and it keeps us physically in trim as well as providing us with a great deal of enjoyment. For those living in moderate climates, tennis is an ideal sport. Unlike golf, which takes the better part of half a day, tennis can be played in an hour's time, early in the morning or after work in the evenings.

The sport's popularity is not without reason. Once it was regarded as primarily for the wealthy, for those who had access to courts through their private clubs. Today, because of its universal appeal and the widespread interest in it, there are courts available in every community, generally without fee. Happily, school courts become accessible in the summer, at the very time when the demand is highest. Even so, in some urban areas access to courts at times may be a problem.

Despite its seeming simplicity, tennis demands constant attempts to improve one's technique. Also, it is a game of strategy, which challenges a player to perform in ways that will cause his opponent to make a bad return. Tennis combines several elements which make it truly one of the great sports: It provides excellent exercise, it constantly challenges us to improve our technique, it sharpens our alertness in developing strategies, and it is great fun.

Tennis, more than most sports, exercises the whole body. Recreational playing, when done several times a week, will keep you feeling fit. It will not totally meet the fitness measure of endurance and aerobic improvement, but combined with jogging or swimming, it should enable one to achieve such fitness. Competitive tennis, on the other hand, when played regularly, may in itself be sufficient to keep fit, for it can be a demanding sport, especially when played as singles.

TENNIS EQUIPMENT. Equipment costs for tennis are relatively low. A good moderate-priced racquet costs $25 or more. Tennis balls are about a dollar apiece. Tennis shoes and socks may cost $20. Therefore, for about $50 one can be well outfitted. Fortunately, unlike skiing, style changes for tennis are few. To be sure new racquet designs are promoted, ranging from improved wooden frames to aluminum, steel, or graphite. Keep in mind that well-designed tennis or athletic shoes will be worth the extra cost, for good foot support and comfort are essential. Less expensive shoes, with arch supports, may serve just as well, but for older people good footwear is advisable.

PHYSICAL REQUIREMENTS.   Tennis is sufficiently demand-ing that you shouldn't play unless you have a doctor's examination and approval. Doing warm-up exercises for a few minutes before beginning play can forestall a pulled muscle. Also, during the first few minutes of the game, avoid reaching for a wide shot. Gracefully concede the point to your opponent.

There is one observation about sports that seems to apply to tennis more than to some other activities. One can take up tennis just for the exercise and for the fun of it. Ultimately, however, it seems to bring out the competitive spirit in a person. As one advances, bad shots or poor control will bring frustrations to the point of disgust. The objective always is to play better. Once you have reached a higher development of technique, the goal is again elevated and the struggle continues. I doubt whether one ever becomes completely satisfied with any level of accomplishment.

GETTING STARTED.   A good way to begin tennis is to go to the nearest court and watch a few games. Also, television carries fascinating professional games, providing some of the most interesting sports fare available. Perhaps a friend will loan you a racquet and some balls, or even take you to a court and show you the fundamentals of the game. It may be unfair, however, to judge your interest in tennis from your first time on the court. Unless you have had experience with some type of racquet game, even ping pong, hitting the ball where you want may be very difficult at first.

There are so many mediocre tennis players, with such a wide range of techniques and form—mostly on the bad side—that you should be encouraged that you can play as well with a little practice. If you don't want to be one of the "horrible examples" you, at the very least, should get a book or two on tennis and study it carefully. If you want to hurry the process, invest in a few lessons from a tennis teacher. Above all, practice as much as possible. Solo hitting of the ball against a blank, flat wall can be very helpful in developing control of your racquet. The effort will be worth it as you thrill with hitting an increasing number of good shots.

Tennis is a game that can be played at any age, from 6 to 80, or even older. John D. Rockefeller, Sr., and King Gustav of Sweden allegedly both played until they were well past 80 years old. So why deprive yourself of all the fun of playing? Start young, shall we say at 50!

One of the appeals of tennis for retired people is that it can be played while traveling. Especially for those who go south in winter months, taking your tennis equipment along requires very little baggage space. If you are driving across the country you will find most small towns and cities will have tennis courts available, without fee. You can take a tennis break occasionally in your traveling, which is good for circulation and muscle tone, if you have been driving long distances. One of the books listed at the end of this chapter (Richards' *Tennis for Travelers*) is a directory of courts available in over 2500 cities, both in the U.S. and abroad. Many entries refer to private clubs, hotels, and motels which have courts, generally with fees. Cross-country travelers, however, need only to pick out small towns to have free access to very good courts in parks and school areas. Several times recently when we went to Colorado to ski, we found the weather so warm that we played tennis a few times instead on courts in city parks. It was a delightful change of pace.

Tennis singles is a somewhat demanding sport for two players. For that reason many older people play doubles (two couples). Doubles is not a game limited to older people, however, for it requires special strategy and good playing. Above all it is great fun, for young or old. It is sufficiently different from singles that there are books and articles published just on doubles. It is a fast game and requires physical and mental dexterity, quick reaction time, close team play, and a special psychology of its own. But, because two people cover the court on each side of the net, it does not require the fast dash across the court that singles often does.

Tennis doubles lends itself to several interesting variations. One can play all male, all female, or mixed doubles. Each combination is different. Men's doubles is a fast, exhausting game, but great fun because of the high competition. Women's doubles is likely to be somewhat slower, and more of a sociable game. Mixed doubles, especially if it is made up of two man–wife teams, can be one of the most enjoyable of your tennis experiences, especially if the couples are roughly equal in ability. For older people it is an ideal game. You can play as hard as you feel like without worrying too much who wins. It provides an interesting social opportunity for couples to join in a common activity. And it is one of the few sports where man and wife can play as partners and, unless they take the game too seriously, enjoy it, even if there is some difference in abilities. If winter trips south or to Hawaii are part of your annual agenda, mixed doubles tennis provides a marvelous recreational opportunity.

Estimates vary as to the number of people playing tennis. Some claim 10 million. Others say there are 24 million serious tennis players in this country, as well as more than 10 million casual players. The A. C. Nielsen Company, a marketing firm, estimated that there were 5 million players in 1960 and over 30 million by 1974, making tennis one of the fastest growing of the participant sports. With this many people vying for courts, you simply have to expect that there will be times when you want to play, only to find all your favorite courts filled. This necessitates planning your tennis games during periods when there is less demand for courts. It also will motivate you to apply political pressure to city hall, to park officials, or to others charged with providing recreational facilities, to recognize the need for more courts.

For many years it has been a mark of distinction to have a swimming pool in your backyard. Perhaps we soon shall see more tennis courts, also. They require considerable space, of course, which will limit installation to homes with very large lots. Also, they are costly to build, probably upwards of $12,000 for some well-surfaced and equipped courts. With such constraints there is not likely to be a mass movement toward courts in private homes.

TIPS FOR PLAYERS OVER 50. Playing tennis is playing tennis, whether one is 20, 50, or 70 years old. The basics are the same, and anyone watching a seniors match is not likely to notice much difference between it and a match played by younger folk. The difference is largely that felt by the players themselves. Older players know they cannot move as quickly as younger ones. They know they may not have the endurance they once had. They are conscious of the fact that they are affected by heat and humidity to a greater degree than younger players. They realize they are more likely to pull a muscle than they used to be.

However, the differences between older players and younger ones are likely to be exaggerated in the minds of many people, young and old alike. Young people are often surprised at "how fast that old duffer can get around." And older people too often assume they cannot get around fast enough and, as a consequence, don't even try to play.

My wife and I had the experience recently of meeting a neighbor just as we were coming back from one of our tennis games. "Oh, do you play tennis?" she exclaimed a bit incredulously. We assured her it was a great game for people our age. "Well, of course it may be for you folks but I'm too old to play tennis," she opined. With a glance at each other my wife and I decided to pursue that point. To our neighbor's great surprise, and our amusement, we determined that she was at least 6 years younger than either of us.

These facts notwithstanding, there are several observations that can be made that will make playing tennis after 50 more enjoyable. Foremost, of course, is to recognize that there are, indeed, changes in physical capabilities as one gets older. One must, therefore, develop a strategem for minimizing these differences.

Perhaps first among the things older tennis players must do is to keep physically fit so that the game does not overtire them. Along with this is the complementary need to conserve as much energy as possible while playing. There are several ways that this can be done which may in fact improve one's game. Tactics are important for all tennis players, but they become an essential for older people. Since one's physical ability to move quickly from one part of the court to another diminishes as one gets older, this must be counterbalanced by strategically placing the ball in the opponent's court to his or her disadvantage. To do this requires good ball control and this comes with much practice. But it is one of the factors that will win games, so it must be emphasized almost from the beginning.

Another energy conservation measure is to avoid trying to return balls that are out of reach. Pursuing such balls will tire one quickly and often is futile anyhow. While there is a satisfaction, and of course an advantage, in successfully returning such balls, perhaps winning the point in the process, in the long run one may become exhausted too soon and lose the set in the end.

There is another point to be made here, however. There is psychological gain in performing beyond the level expected of people your age. It helps dispel the general attitude that some people are too old to play effectively. Then, too, one may gain, at least temporarily, a mental lift from the exhilaration of having successfully returned a difficult retrieve. This is important in the general improvement of one's own psychological state simply because tennis, like many other sports, is a game that depends on one's self-esteem. It is easy to become "psyched out," as some say, and at that point one is a sure loser. The opposite holds also, and books on "inner tennis" stress the importance of a correct positive mental attitude while playing.

Older tennis players also conserve their energy by playing more doubles than singles. Probably half the energy of singles is required for doubles and, fortunately, doubles are equally enjoyable for many. Playing during the cool part of the day rather than when the sun is at its peak also will be less tiring. Heat and bright sun are enervating in themselves and playing at midday simply is more exhausting.

A wise older sportsman is one who knows and respects the limits of his ability, endurance, and physical capacity. There is no shame in declaring that you have reached the point at which you must rest. Better to save yourself to play another time rather than overdoing it to avoid admitting you are tired or getting too warm. It is important that you stop occasionally during play for a breather and for replenishment of the liquid you have lost. A small amount of water or other refreshment should be taken periodically, such as between sets, to avoid dehydration, and consequent headache in the bargain, perhaps.

Another factor that will help older players win points and games, of course, is good technique. For example, developing an effective

Vic Seixas, 55, has played 55 Davis Cup matches—more than any other Ameri-can. Here he approaches the net in perfect position to hit a return volley. As he closely watches the ball, his racquet is extended in front of him to meet the ball squarely.

serve is a major advantage. A well-executed slice or top spin on a serve puts the receiver at an immediate disadvantage. A slice pulls him out of position or off balance, and chances are, if he returns the ball at all, it will be in a position for you to easily put it away to score the point. A top spin is a difficult ball to handle, in my judgment, for it not only lurches forward faster as it hits the surface, it also veers to the side. Some older people have trouble delivering a top-spin serve, however, for it requires handling the racquet in such a way that it puts a special strain on one's back. I, for one, cannot use it because of my history of a disc problem.

As one gets older one does have to make some adjustments in the way the game is played. But it should be apparent that these adjustments are neither radical nor demeaning, nor do they diminish the enjoyment of playing. Indeed, they may even enhance one's game. Hitting a cannon ball return, which few people do well anyhow, is no more fun than hitting a strategically placed return. A well-developed and executed tactical game is more impressive, in my opinion, than a game with power returns and mad dashes back and forth on the court.

FOR MORE INFORMATION

Tennis, like many sports, can be learned from books and reading, as far as fundamentals, techniques, rules, and strategies are concerned. But there is only one way to develop your ability to play, and that is by playing, and playing often. Like skiing, it will take a couple of years of earnest practice before you begin to be satisfied with your progress. But you will have fun in the process, and the exercise will make you feel great. Your only regret will be that you hadn't started sooner. So, to begin your tennis adventure, look at some books and magazines. As an example of what is available, I have listed below a selection of titles that will be both interesting and instructive.

Books:

All About Tennis. Chicago, Rand McNally, 1975. $4.95.
> A readable, well-illustrated book especially for the beginner. Covers instruction, equipment, a directory of tennis clinics, a who's who in tennis, and tennis records set.

Amdur, Neil. *Tennis Guide.* Clearwater, Fl., Snibbe Publications, Annual. $1.00.
> Handy pocket or purse-sized guide that covers the essentials, with many valuable tips. Has only a few illustrations. Easily worth the cost.

Gonzales, Pancho. *Tennis Begins at Forty.* New York, Dial Press, 1976. $12.95.
> Overpriced, and does not contribute that much that is new about the older player.

Johnson, J. D., and P. J. Xanthos. *Tennis.* 2nd Ed. Dubuque, Ia., Wm. C. Brown, 1972. $2.50.
> Good instructive basic guide with illustrations.

Mason, R. Elaine. *Tennis.* Boston, Allyn & Bacon, 1974. $2.95.
> Thorough guide for the beginner as well as the experienced player.

Metzler, Paul. *Tennis Doubles: Tactics & Formations.* New York, Cornerstone Library, 1975. $1.95.
> Excellent for development of strategy, the key to success in playing doubles.

Richards, Gilbert. *Tennis for Travelers.* 4th Ed. Cincinnati, Tennis for Travelers, 1973. $6.00.
> A directory of available courts in the United States and abroad; primarily refers to motels, resorts, hotels, and clubs. Does not attempt to list publicly available courts in parks that any traveler can use.

Smith, Stan. *Inside Tennis.* Chicago, Regnery, 1974. $4.95.
> One of the best books for beginners. It is simply explained and very well illustrated.

Magazines:

Eastern Tennis. Quarterly. 420 Lexington Avenue, Room 2540, New York 10017. $4.00 per year.

Tennis. Monthly. Tennis Features, Inc., 495 Westport Avenue, Norwalk, Ct. 06856. $9.50 per year.

Tennis Illustrated. Monthly. Devonshire Publications, 630 Shatto Place, Los Angeles, Ca. 90005. $7.00 per year.

Tennis USA. Monthly. Chilton Co., Radnor, Pa. 19089. Published for the United States Lawn Tennis Association. $7.00 per year.

15 *Golf*

I F YOU HAVE not experienced an early morning outing on the golf course, you simply owe it to yourself to try it. Few competitive sports offer such delightful surroundings. The well-trimmed grass fairways and manicured greens, the rolling hills, the trees, and perhaps a view of a lake or seaside, combine to provide golf with a luxurious setting.

Golf is a game particularly appropriate for those over 50. It is especially attractive for retired people who have the time to spend a half day playing. And for those with physical handicaps, golf carts offer one of the few opportunities to participate in a competitive sport that can be exciting, enjoyable, and thoroughly rewarding.

Age, while affecting certain aspects of how one plays, may actually improve your game. Adjustments in the swing, the weight of the clubs, and the particular club used for a certain shot should compensate for loss of power in the swing. Apparently George H. Miller of Anaheim, California, made the correct adjustments for, at 93, he set the record as the oldest person to make a hole-in-one. Edna Hussey of Cincinnati also set a record for women, making a hole-in-one at 81 years of age. Apparently golfing knows no age limits. Perhaps the slogan of the U.S. National Senior Open Golf Association is one that can be applied more widely than just to golf. It is, "You don't stop playing because you grow old; you grow old because you stop playing."

Golfing is indulgent with respect to competency. There isn't a breathing golfer, even among professionals, who hasn't been deflated from time to time by making an unbelievably bad drive or putt. One of the attractive features of golf is that, while it is a game of competition among fellow golfers, it is also a challenge to one's own abilities. One strives constantly to improve previous scores, pitted against the course and himself, and only secondarily against fellow golfers. Through the handicap system two golfers of different abilities can play and enjoy themselves on an equal status. This makes the game especially attractive to husbands and wives who can play without any embarrassment because of one partner's lack of skill or ability.

BASICS OF GOLF. There are various opportunities available for the would-be golfer. One can play public golf courses simply by paying the required fee. Almost every municipality has such a course available. Or one can belong to a country club, a private organization that may have many activities in addition to golf, for which relatively high annual membership dues are charged. In between these extremes are other courses, such as those at resorts and those supported by private companies or educational institutions.

My experience as a golfer has been an on-and-off thing over the years. I played some, simply for pleasure, as a graduate student. Since then I normally have participated in an annual outing among my colleagues at work. My most enjoyable golf was played when my wife and I took a winter trip south several years ago. Each day we would play the nearby public course, enjoying to the fullest the warm sunshine and the contrast to what we had just left in Minnesota. Amidst the palm trees we drove and putted badly, true duffers that we were, but relishing every minute of it.

The basics of golf are relatively simple to understand. Sometimes it appears that protocol and etiquette dominate the game, but there are rules to be learned also. A time or two out on the course with golfing friends will teach you the fundamentals. It is both a delightful and a frustrating game for the beginner. One thrills with the occasional good drive or putt that even the novice will make. But more likely one is apt to experience disgust for the first few times out because of the preciseness required in hitting the golf ball consistently.

Particularly at first one is well advised to visit a driving range a few times. There one can rent a bucket of balls and practice driving them. In golf, as in so many sports, a few lessons at the beginning will pay dividends. Habits formed at the start should be good habits, not bad ones. Once bad form is adopted as a way of playing it is doubly difficult to correct it. Competent instruction from a golf pro can sometimes produce startling results. Joseph Gambatese, in *Golf Guide*, advises at least 6 half-hour lessons. Private lessons are better than group lessons but, of course, cost more. "Learn to play, rather than play to learn," says Lional Callaway.

Golf, more than many sports, is a psychological game. It is a game of concentration. If you have watched the pro matches on television you have noted that the crowd, even the commentator, all remain silent when the golfer is about to tee off down the fairway or putt on the green. One's game is also affected by mental attitudes. Disgust or frustration often leads to poorer scores. Carelessness and casualness will not win games. Indecisiveness or lack of forethought as one plans the drive or putt is likely to result in poor performance. Self-analysis of why you are making bad (or good) strokes is essential for improvement. While all this may sound a bit ominous, many, if not most, recreational golfers simply enjoy the game, although they are constantly trying to better their previous scores.

Begin your golfing by watching professional tournaments on television. Although golf is a rather slow-moving game, it is interesting to see how the experts play. If you have a color TV set you can see the beautiful surroundings in which golf is played. Watching is a good way to learn the fundamentals of the game, at least the finer points. But to understand what you are seeing you should at least read and understand the basic rules of golf beforehand.

The golfer pivots to complete his drive. Although the club extends properly on the follow-through, his weight should transfer more to his left foot, and he should not look up too quickly while hitting the ball.

EQUIPMENT FOR GOLFING.   Experts advise those just beginning golf to rent a set of clubs for your first few times out. This does have some advantages. First, there is a chance that the game won't appeal to you, and you will not have invested in clubs you won't use. Also, if you use several different sets of clubs you will begin to have preferences that will be helpful when you make your selection for purchase.

When you are ready to buy your clubs, visit with the golf pro at a nearby golf course. He may have a used set that someone traded in that will be suitable for you. Chances are you will get a better set for the money than if you buy new ones. Golf clubs do not wear out, although a shaft can be bent. Check over the used set carefully for damage.

Clubs come in matched sets, usually bearing the names of golfing personalities, which imply endorsement of the set. Your concern should not be the prestige name but rather the characteristics of the clubs and their suitability for your particular needs. Even experienced players have difficulty in selecting clubs, so seek all the advice you can get. You wouldn't want a very flexible, fast action shaft if you need a stiff one, nor a heavyweight clubhead when you require a light one. If you do not have access to a golf pro, check with a reputable sporting goods store for advice.

In addition to your clubs you will need a bag to carry them in. If you plan to carry your own clubs over the fairway, there is a distinct advantage in a lightweight bag, although it won't be as durable as a leather one. Also, if you plan to buy a full set of clubs, you will need a large bag, whereas a limited set will fit in a slimmer one. On the other hand, if you always plan to use a golf cart anyhow, a large sturdy bag has advantages.

As somewhat of a duffer who believes in golf not only as a fun sport, but also as a means of keeping physically fit, I shun riding golf carts. Unless you are handicapped or old and feeble, I firmly believe you should walk fairways, carrying your own bag or using a golf caddy cart. It definitely is more enjoyable, but then I thoroughly enjoy walking, especially in such beautiful surroundings. It follows, then, that I also believe you should have the minimum number of clubs, especially in the beginning. You can then get by with a small golf bag. Adopting this philosophy, of course, reduces the cost of equipment. Also walking rather than renting a golf cart lowers the cost of each game. However, some private golf courses require the use of golf carts to speed up the game, in which case, if you choose to play there, you will have to use a cart.

In addition to clubs and a bag, you will need golf balls. They are precision made and relatively expensive. Unfortunately, beginners are more prone to making wild drives into the rough or into water hazards, where balls are often lost. These are costly mistakes, and several such drives in a game will convince you that a few lessons and time at a driving range practicing your drives will be well worth the cost. Undoubtedly you will have opportunities (you needn't look for them, they will find you!) to buy used golf balls. Enterprising youngsters search out-of-bounds areas for balls or fish them from water hazards. If you select those that have not been damaged, these can save you some money. Once you are known to be a golfer you will find that gifts of golf balls for birthdays or other occasions are quite appropriate and some may come your way.

Experienced golfers often wear golf shoes. These are oxfords with spikes and are generally worn by those who walk the fairways rather than ride the carts. They make walking easier, reducing slippage. I have never owned a pair. I wear crepe-soled shoes and have had no problem. It is a decision you needn't make at the outset.

Other clothes are a matter of personal preference. Ultimately, you will want to buy some "appropriate" golf clothes, but don't rush into outfitting yourself with the latest in golf attire. See what others are wearing first. Perhaps you may not even buy anything special once you get into the game. An umbrella might be useful. If you get caught on the fairway in a sudden downpour, there isn't much of any place to go for shelter, and heading for a tree is a bad decision, especially if there is lightning.

Golf is a relatively expensive sport for the recreational player. Like photography, it is expensive not because of the original outlay for equipment, but because of the cost of using it. Nevertheless, an estimated 12 million Americans are playing golf on some 10,000 courses in the United States. The initial investment in equipment is about equivalent to the cost of a color television set. And each time you play a public course it will cost you what you would pay for a modest dinner. Forego the dinner and play golf. It probably will be better for you.

PHYSICAL PREPARATION. One of the great appeals of golf to older people is that it is not a strenuous sport. One does a moderate amount of exercising on the course, to be sure, especially if you walk rather than ride the golf cart. But the sport is not a demanding one, physically.

To get some idea what is involved, one can make some simple computations. Courses will vary in length, but generally for 18 holes one will walk more than 4 miles, maybe as many as 6. This will be over turf that is firm, but the course is likely to go up and down over gentle slopes. Putting is about as effortless as croquet once you are on the green. To get to a green may require 4 or more vigorous swings for a beginner. In 18 holes, therefore, one will swing a club some 6 dozen times. If you are not in reasonably good physical condition, an 18-hole game will be quite tiring, and your arm and shoulder muscles will feel the strain. Also, because one grips the clubs tightly, hand muscles will fatigue unless they are conditioned beforehand. Some golfers keep a rubber ball around and practice squeezing it several times daily to strengthen their hand muscles.

Walking 4 to 6 miles in a half day, in addition to the many swings required, adds up to considerable exercise. Many beginners will start out playing 9 holes only. There isn't anything in between 9 and 18, so the decision to go the last 9 is a big one. That is not to say that you can't stop any place along the second 9, but if you are playing a twosome or foursome, it is a little awkward to drop out midway. Better to prepare physically beforehand for what is involved. You will enjoy the game more and probably even play better.

To approach the green with a short iron, notice that the player has choked up on the club and shortened his swing for shorter distance. While his feet are comfortably apart, he should bend his knees more, rather than leaning over the ball.

Golfers claim that one's legs are the first things to give out. Therefore, keeping your legs in good physical condition through a regimen of jogging should be especially beneficial for golfing. I find that the swinging of golf clubs during drives is the most strain for me, perhaps because it pulls the back muscles. For me proper back conditioning is essential. If you have any medical record of back problems, it would be well for you to check with your doctor before taking up golf. This is especially important the older one becomes.

TIPS FOR OLDER GOLFERS.   While I personally prefer to walk the fairways rather than ride a golf cart, one should recognize that to walk the distance required for an 18-hole game may not be prudent for many older players. Riding the cart may be a necessity. My brother, who took up golf mostly since he retired some years ago, and now plays almost daily, has maintained his fit condition even though he rides the cart. He reminds me that getting in and out of the cart, perhaps as often as 60 times in the course of the game, is in itself considerable exercise. This, combined with the 6 dozen or more hard swings of the golf club, and the jostling over the fairways in the cart, all add up to more activity than one might at first assume.

One of the most extraordinary golfers I have observed was an elderly man with no legs who played golf frequently. He rode in a golf cart with another person who did the driving. He would negotiate his game from the cart and made rather remarkable drives while seated. He was willing to forego the part of the game that occurs on the greens. The important point is that he participated, despite what for many would be a total disability. Older golfers should not give up lightly the opportunity to play golf since, with resolve, one often can work out methods of accommodation to even severe handicaps.

One of the advantages the older retired golfer has over younger ones still in their work years is better access to the golf course. Weekends find courses crowded. Also, often in an attempt to control overcrowding, course operators will raise the greens fees on Saturdays and Sundays. Retired golfers can arrange golf outings during the week, saving both time and money, as well as a good deal of frustration waiting for their turn to start.

Golf, like many sports, is a psychological game. Older golfers new to the game should recognize at the outset that getting the muscles to react nimbly and precisely will take considerably longer than it might have in younger years. One's form is likely to be somewhat less than perfect, certainly at the beginning. Indeed, it may never achieve the ideal. Accepting that fact at the outset will go a long way to promoting a healthy, unperturbed attitude so essential to playing a satisfactory game. One also has to recognize that the score achieved by older players new to the game may never be spectacular. The important thing is to enjoy the game, relax, drink in the beauty of the outdoor surroundings, and establish friendships with fellow players who have similar goals. Modest goals achieved are far more enjoyable than high goals thwarted and agonized about. Chances are very good that whatever high scores (which in golf are at the losing end of the scale!) an older player makes are likely to be due to factors other than age. One's posture, swing, club, mental attitude, amount of practice and playing—all are probably more critical than the fact that one has reached the age of 60 or more.

In recognition of the fact that anyone over 50 beginning golf simply has fewer years to play and therefore less time to develop himself into a first-rate player, it behooves one to speed up the process of learning to play well. One way that this can be done, of course, is to take lessons. Some universities and colleges offer golf as an extension course. Anyone over 60 may be able to register for the course free or at little cost—one of the increasing number of advantages of getting old! In addition, it is very helpful to hit a bucket of balls at a golf practice range, which can be located through the yellow pages of a telephone directory. It is especially useful to take a friend along who is a golfer, so that he or she can watch your swings and drives and offer suggestions for your improvement.

Because golfing is one of the most popular recreational sports, appealing to many who may not have other athletic abilities, many books and magazines are published on golf. Any good book on golfing will describe the fundamentals of the game. After you begin playing, it is interesting to read a golf magazine to learn about new equipment, styles, and golfing news happenings, and perhaps pick up some hints on improving your game.

FOR MORE INFORMATION

Below is a sample of publications available. You can obtain these or similar titles at your local public library or purchase them through a bookstore or sporting goods shop.

Books:
All About Golf. Skokie, Ill., Rand McNally, 1975. $4.95.
 Presents history of golf, fundamentals, techniques of playing, golfing records, people in golf, and equipment suggestions.
Ford, Doug. *Getting Started in Golf.* New York, Cornerstone, 1964. $1.95.
 Easy guide for a beginner to use. Stresses fundamentals.
Gambatese, Joseph. *Golf Guide.* Clearwater, Fl., Snibbe Publications. Annual. $1.00.
 Very convenient, small pocket guide to many facts, techniques, equipment, and playing suggestions.

———, ed. *Gene Sarazen's World Golf Dictionary*, 1721 DeSales St., NW, Washington, D.C. 20036. $7.50.

Lists over 1600 golf courses with information on score cards, layouts, and other facts.

Gunn, Dr. Harry E. (Bud), and Earl Stewart, Jr. *Golf Begins at 40*. Matteson, Ill., Greatlakes Living Press, 1977. $5.95.

Nance, Virginia L., and Elwood Craig Davis. *Golf*. 3rd Ed. Dubuque, Ia., Wm. C. Brown, 1975. $2.50.

Logical, step-by-step instruction book to teach fundamentals.

The Offical Rules of Golf. United States Golf Association, 40 East 38th St., New York, 1972.

Runyon, Paul. *Paul Runyon's Book for Senior Golfers*. New York, Dodd Mead, 1963. $4.50.

Sarazen, Gene. *Better Golf After Fifty*. New York, Harper & Row, 1967. $7.95.

Magazines:

Golf. Monthly. Times-Mirror Magazines, Inc., 380 Madison Ave., New York 10017. $7.95 per year.

Golf Journal. 10 times per year. The official publication of the U.S. Golf Association. Published by the Chilton Co., Radnor, Pa. 19089. $3.50 per year.

Golf/USA. Monthly. Southern Golfer Publishing Co., Box 2102, Jackson, Ms. 39205. $6.00 per year.

Senior Golfer. Quarterly. Senior Golf Publications Co., Box 4716, Clearwater, Fl. 33518. $2.50 per year.

The only magazine edited exclusively for the over-50 golfer. Reports activities and calendar of events for senior golfing organizations throughout the U.S. Also serves as reporter for the U.S. National Senior Open Golf Association.

16   *Horseback Riding*

S PORTSMEN are always pleased when a U.S. President associates himself with a favorite sport. Thus golf (Eisenhower), walking (Truman), sailing and touch football (Kennedy), skiing and swimming (Ford), canoeing and kayaking (Carter), all have had their presidential advocates. Although Lyndon Johnson, as a rancher, rode horses, the President most often thought of as a horseback rider was Calvin Coolidge. And, of course, Teddy Roosevelt before him.

As an enjoyable form of exercise, horseback riding has many unique aspects. Among its great advantages is that riding can take one into beautiful and otherwise inaccessible areas. Guided pack trips in mountainous states, while fairly expensive, can be marvelous adventures. While my wife and I are not regular riders today—not because we don't enjoy the sport, but mainly because we can't seem to work it in with all our other activities—we are no strangers to riding. I rode horses almost every day from the time I could walk until I was a young man. Riding for city folk is not an easy thing to arrange, especially when one does not live in a particularly horsey area. If we lived in Colorado, you can bet we would be regular riders.

Among our most unusual horseback riding experiences was the one in Egypt, just outside Cairo. By chance we had met an American author while dining in Cairo. She told of her plan to go riding on the desert the next morning and invited us to join her, an invitation we delightedly accepted. She picked us up at our hotel the next morning and we proceeded to what passes as a stable in Egypt. There an affable, garrulous, nomadic type met us. We were to learn that he had allegedly ridden in the film about Lawrence of Arabia. He supplied each of us with a mount he judged suitable. Mine was a feisty Arabian that I had difficulty keeping in check. Once mounted we headed for the desert, with our Egyptian friend serving as our guide. Mid-morning we were riding in the vicinity of the Pyramids, a most unusual experience to say the least. Unlike other tourists, we were out on the desert where we could see a number of smaller pyramids behind the Great Pyramid. We also saw the Sphinx and Great Pyramid at angles not seen by other tourists. One of the pictures we treasure is of our son, who put on the *jalabiyah* (robe) of our Egyptian friend and, astride his horse, with the pyramids in the background, posed as a make-believe nomad. Of the many hundreds of photographs I have taken over the years, I count this as one of my all-time favorites.

In writing this book, I have not only drawn upon my personal experiences but also have read many books and magazines about the various sports discussed. I have been impressed with the number of times writers proclaim mushrooming interest in their particular sport. That claim probably is less true of horseback riding. However, I predict that the interest will grow in coming years. Horseback riding facilities are becoming more available. This is particularly noticeable where there are seasonal activity resorts. For example, many ski resorts now have summer family programs that compare favorably with their wintertime offerings. Resort owners, to survive economically and to maximize the use of their expensive and costly-to-maintain facilities, have broadened their programs to include year-round activities. Many have added a stable of horses, a wrangler, trails, and pack outings.

Dude ranches have existed for many years, of course, but it appears that they, too, have taken on new life and continue to be the most popular form of horseback vacation. Dude ranches are basically horse-centered resorts. The staff concentrates on providing guests with a good time. The primary activity is riding, but there are also swimming, tennis, and dancing. Activities are geared, of course, to those who enjoy resorts.

The family ranch, which welcomes paying guests, is another opportunity for horseback riding. Here one might become one of the ranch hands, helping with farm and ranch chores and daily activities, such as herding grazing cattle. Guests become a part of the family for a week and are treated as such. It could be a welcome change from city life, especially for those who have never had rural experience.

For the more adventurous outdoorsmen the pack trip may have some appeal. This kind of outing is usually under the supervision of a guide, with provisions and pack horses a part of the package. Aside from this, the experience will have some similarity to backpacking. You will live out-of-doors for a few days, see scenery not available to most tourists, and experience nature at its best—in the raw.

Information on dude ranches and pack trip ranches can be obtained from the Dude Ranch Association, P.O. Box 1363, Billings, Montana 59103. In making inquiries, be as specific as you can as to your interest so that pertinent information can be sent to you. The Sierra Club, known for its many outdoor activities, includes pack trip excursions among its offerings. Many other naturalist-type organizations may have information useful for the would-be horseback rider. Your library can serve as a useful information center for the names and addresses of such organizations as well as books on riding, wilderness travel, camping, and packing.

A related activity, albeit a spectator event, is the western rodeo. Found primarily west of the Mississippi River, rodeos can introduce you to the potentialities of horseback riding, although, truthfully, few of us are likely to want seriously to participate in this rough and tumble activity. Nevertheless, dude ranches often offer guests the opportunity for some rodeo antics, including handling of the lariat. If you are good enough you may even want to try your hand at roping a calf.

Rodeos in Wyoming, Montana, Colorado, Nebraska, Iowa, and many other states, are the United States' counterpart to the bull-fights of Spain and Mexico. We pretend to be more humane in the treatment of our animals, of course. Nevertheless, you may gasp a little the first time you watch the calf-roping event, especially at the moment the calf is suddenly wrenched to the ground by a tight rope as he is bounding away. Although I have seen a number of rodeos, I have yet to see an injured animal. But I've seen a few injured cowboys. Unlike the bullfight, therefore, I'm inclined to think the rodeo's odds are in favor of the animals.

At a rodeo we recently attended in Wyoming, there was a break in the program during which the audience, numbering 50 or so people, was invited to come over to the corrals and have a closer look at the broncos, equipment, and other animals. Cowboys explained how the release chutes worked, the characteristics of good rodeo horses, and their value, and answered questions. One piece of information of interest to those who may be contemplating buying their own horses is the fact that a good horse can cost as much as a new automobile. And, like photography, it may not be the initial cost that is the important one. The care and feeding of horses is of a dimension not to be taken casually.

For most of us horseback riding will be a now-and-then activity, provided mostly by public riding facilities in national parks and forests, or some state, county, and city parks. There are similar facilities in Canada. Many private resorts also offer riding as a part of their programs. Books on riding vacations, such as the Steven Price book, listed below, have directories of riding facilities in various areas.

There are other sports associated with horseback riding which most of us will be content to watch. These usually require excellent riding abilities as well as other skills. I recall a pleasant Sunday afternoon a few years ago watching a polo game in Chicago. It obviously is not for amateurs, but it is a fast-moving, interesting sport, with beautiful animals performing superbly. Fox hunting, although thought of as an English sport, is alive also in the United States. It is estimated that there are some 140 hunt packs in the United States and Canada today. Then there are the activities that display horsemanship, such as horse shows and steeplechase competition.

Although we have had one experience riding abroad, as described before, I could not help but be intrigued by Steven Price's description of riding opportunities in the British Isles. Riding in Ireland is now on my list of things I want to do someday. What could be more pleasant than riding over the green Irish countryside, or through Robin Hood's Sherwood Forest?

If you want to see a dressage performance unrivalled anywhere else in the world, visit the Spanish Riding School in Vienna. There the riders, in a tradition of long standing, will put their famed

Lippizaners through routines with such precision that it will astonish and amaze you.

This chapter would not be complete without including the suggestion to watch a horse race. Statistics indicate that more people go to horse races than attend football or baseball games. Is it because of the element of betting, the thrill of the possibility of winning? Also, is that the reason so little is heard about horse racing, as compared to other sports? The closest we have come to seeing a major horse race in person was the time we visited Churchill Downs in Louisville, Kentucky. We later watched the Kentucky Derby on television. One can easily get caught up in this spectator sport even if no betting is involved.

There are other aspects to the many-sided sport of horseback riding. It is safe to say that America's fondness for horses has not dwindled, and every indication is that horses will become more and more common. Calvin Coolidge regarded riding as an excellent and pleasurable form of exercise. If you haven't experienced it, you ought to try it. You may well agree with him.

TIPS FOR OLDER HORSEBACK RIDERS. If you have never ridden a horse, you have some surprises in store. No doubt you will feel as I did when I first rode a camel in Egypt. Until one learns how to ride, it can be a pretty bumpy affair. For my part I'll leave the camels to the Arabs and Egyptians. But riding a horse properly can be a relatively smooth experience, providing the horse cooperates, of course, and doesn't insist on trotting part of the time.

One of the surprises waiting for you will be the day after your first ride. It is enough to make you vow never to ride again! Straddling a horse spreads your legs in a very unnatural way, and your large leg muscles are almost sure to be very sore the next day. If you are planning a pack trip, I would certainly urge you to ride for a few days beforehand so that your legs will become accustomed to the strain. If you don't, it may ruin your outing. You may have a better appreciation of the alleged bowed legs of cowboys after your first experience at riding!

Some of our most beautiful country is in remote places where there are no roads, and thus it is not seen by very many people. One way to see such places, of course, is to backpack in over established foot trails. But some of us may not have the equipment, the energy, the desire, or, for that matter, even the capacity and health for such exertion. In places where there are pack trails and suitable outfitters, horsebacking in offers an option that most people can use. For example, one of the places well worth seeing is the bottom of the Grand Canyon. Bearing in mind that the canyon is a mile deep, and the heat on the trail to and from the bottom is intense, older people have only one way to get down to see this phenomenon, and that is by pack mule or horseback. Walking down would be foolhardy and only the fittest of even young people should attempt it. There are no roads, and helicopters are usually used for emergencies and are too expensive for most of us. Although I haven't done it, I know enough about horseback riding to believe that the trip down into the Canyon and back may not be among your most enjoyable riding experiences. Nevertheless, it does open up an opportunity to see something that is foreclosed to you by almost any other means.

If you are riding for the first time, you should inform the wrangler of this so that he can select a mount suitable for you. Some horses are more nervous and excitable than others. Some will be champing at the bit constantly and to hold such horses in check can become tiring and take some of the pleasure out of riding. In other words, there should be a match between the horse and rider. Should you be fortunate enough to get the right horse, be prepared to become quite attached to him. Horses are great animals. It might even start you dreaming as to how you might manage to get a place where you could have your own horse.

FOR MORE INFORMATION

There are a number of books on riding. Check with your bookstore or public library for the following, or other titles that will provide you with detailed information.

Books:

DeRomaszkan, Gregor. *Fundamentals of Riding.* New York, Doubleday. $5.50.

Heath, Veronica. *Beginner's Guide to Riding.* New York, Transatlantic, 1971. $7.50.

Hundt, Sheila W. *Invitation to Riding.* New York, Simon & Schuster, 1976. $9.95.

Hyland, Ann. *Beginner's Guide to Western Riding.* New York, Transatlantic, 1972. $7.50.

Merrill, Bill. *Vacationing with Saddle and Packhorse.* New York, Arco, 1977. $3.95.

Price, Steven D. *Horseback Vacation Guide.* Brattleboro, Vt. The Stephen Greene Press, 1975. $5.95.
A first-rate beginner's book on all sorts of riding adventures, as a participant or as a spectator at sporting events. Includes directories to guide the reader to more specific information.

Sports Illustrated Horseback Riding. New York, Lippincott, 1971. $1.95.

Magazines:

Horse & Rider. Monthly. Rich Publishing, Inc., Box 555, Temecula, Ca. 92390. $7.00 per year.

Horseman; the Magazine of Western Riding. Monthly. Cordovan Corp., 5314 Bingle Road, Houston, Tex. 77018. $7.00 per year.

17 *Hiking and Backpacking*

I F ONE WERE to classify the various activities described in this book, one would put in the same general category *walking, hiking,* and *backpacking*. The difference among them is largely a matter of degree. All three depend on walking as a basic function. I could have appropriately combined *walking* and *hiking*. Rather I've chosen to discuss *hiking* along with *backpacking*, for both are so interrelated that a separate discussion of each will inevitably lead to redundancy.

Hiking differs from walking primarily in where one goes for the jaunt and the length of time spent at it. Walking rapidly all day over the trails in the Rocky Mountain National Park could properly be called *hiking*. But hiking around a city park lake for an hour is really *walking*. A decision to go hiking and backpacking is a fairly major one, requiring advance preparation and usually travel to some wilderness or coastal area.

One's incentive for hiking and backpacking can either be love or hate: love and longing for peace and solitude, the clean air, the sounds of the wild, the beautiful scenery; or hate of the noise and distractions of the city, the polluted atmosphere, the blaring television, the stresses of the office, or the snarled traffic jams. Solitude, as Sigurd F. Olson wrote in his book, *Reflections from the North Country*, leads to an awakening of ideas and thoughts normally hidden when one is with others and concepts emerge which otherwise are lost in interruptions and responsibilities. Solitude, he says, is "understood only when we have been without it."

Backpacking also has much in common with wilderness canoeing. Both require packing along food and shelter and other necessities of living. Both depend on camping expertise. Either activity necessitates careful planning and preparation. For safety's sake, one should study the maps of the routes or trails, know what to do in emergencies, and notify rangers or outfitters when you are going, the route you plan to take, and how long you estimate you will be out. Should you not return within a reasonable time of your estimate, searchers probably will be sent out to determine why.

Backpacking offers a variety of pleasures denied other campers, particularly automobile campers. Mountain trails lead to some of the best trout fishing available. Pristine mountain lakes reachable only on foot do not suffer from overuse as do so many of our lakes. It is only a small percentage of our peripatetic anglers who are willing to backpack to remote fishing spots to enjoy their sport. For those who want to get away from the crowd, the National Forests alone provide over 3 million acres of lake waters and 81,000 miles of fishing streams.

Some hikers head for the mountain trails to hunt. The U.S. Forest

Service provides ample opportunity, on unposted land, to hunt a variety of big game animals. The best hunting, however, is likely to be with the camera. Spectacular vistas captivate hikers and backpackers as they reach summits along the trail. However, only the mind's eye, not the camera, will do justice to the views. The armchair hiker, even though he may vicariously enjoy the scenery in beautiful photos, will never fully know and appreciate it as will those who have the live experience.

WHERE TO GO. There may be valid reasons for not going hiking or backpacking. However, not having a place to go cannot be one of them. Fortunately, there is mounting interest among many local groups in establishing and maintaining hiking trails in their areas. Nationally and regionally there are longstanding clubs, such as the Sierra Club, dedicated to promoting the enjoyment of wilderness areas. The U.S. Forest Service has well over 100,000 miles of maintained trails and millions of acres of roadless area open to hikers. The national park system has some 12,000 miles of trails through scenic areas. The Appalachian Mountain Trail, for example, extends some 2000 miles from Maine to Georgia over some beautifully wooded terrain. Contrary to what some people believe, nearly 1/3 of our land area in the United States is in the public domain controlled by the federal government. This is your and my land, to be used for our enjoyment.

Canada has a trail system that offers endless opportunity for hiking. Some of the plans for extending the U.S. trails include hooking up with Canadian trails. The U.S. plans include a network of trails which ultimately will put hiking areas in or near almost any state. The Pacific Crest National Scenic Trail, for example, reaches from Canada to the Mexican border, a distance of some 2400 miles. Other major trail systems planned or completed will criss-cross the nation, often covering historic routes. Among these are old cattle trails in the southwest, the Lewis and Clark Trail, the Oregon Trail, the Mormon Trail, and the Gold Rush Trail in Alaska.

CLUBS AND ORGANIZATIONS. Hikers, nature lovers, and backpackers have a plethora of organizations to assist would-be participants. The Wilderness Society conducts group trips led by experienced guides. The Sierra Club, with its local chapters, offers the beginner guidance and enthusiasm, as well as exerting social and political pressure to maintain our natural surroundings. Its "Totebooks," listed at the end of this chapter, are useful as well as interesting reading. The Appalachian Mountain Club assists in preparing, marking, and maintaining trails. Most regions or large urban areas have local nature clubs or branches of national organizations, such as the Audubon Society.

EQUIPMENT NEEDED. Throughout this book I have urged the use of proper equipment as a prerequisite to enjoying various activities. Especially, I have stressed the necessity of good footwear for people as they get older. No other sport is as dependent on good footwear as is backpacking. "Feet are basic" could be a backpacker's motto. Sporting goods manufacturers offer a variety of sturdy hiking shoes, cleated to provide good traction, with heavy soles to guard against bruises from rocks and stones along the trail.

Backpacks must be planned very carefully. A pack frame eases the carrying but the fundamental requirement is to plan well, keep the gear to the bare essentials, and use as lightweight equipment as can be found. If properly planned, a backpacker's week-long load including food, utensils, sleeping bag, clothes, etc., can be kept to no more than 25 pounds. A good guidebook should be carefully studied to note essential items needed, quantities, sources of supply, and

Mount Eisenhower in the New Hampshire Presidential Range. Note the walking stick for balance in rocky, uneven terrain. Always be prepared for sudden and extreme changes in weather at high altitudes. Piles of stones, or "cairns," mark the trail.

directions for getting trail maps and identifying the locations of maintained trails.

A down-filled sleeping bag is excellent for several reasons. It rolls to a small pack for ease in carrying. It is lightweight. It is warm. I might add also that it is relatively expensive. But the extra cost will not add that large an increment to your total trip cost. Should you try to economize, you may wish you hadn't if you are trying to get some much-needed sleep in below-freezing temperatures in the mountains. As we get older it appears to be increasingly unpleasant to be cold while sleeping.

The nylon pup tent is ideal for backpacking. It is strong yet very lightweight. It sheds water and dries rapidly if it gets wet, as it almost inevitably will in the mountains. Some backpackers prefer to sleep under the stars, perhaps taking a lightweight tarp to protect against rain. That may be romantic, but it is not my preference.

For those who do not wish to invest in equipment, there are outfitters who can provide all necessities. Whether you buy or rent equipment largely depends on how often you expect to use it. For a one-time jaunt, renting undoubtedly is the answer. If there are others in your family who can use the gear, you should also bear in mind that most camping equipment of good quality will last many years if properly cared for.

ORIENTEERING.   There recently has occurred a new sport in this country that is an essential part of the canoer's, hiker's, and backpacker's knowledge. It is called "orienteering." It has to do with one's ability to read maps, determine directions, study and use topographical features, and generally remain properly oriented—that is, know where one is at all times. For backpacking hikes it is essential to have this skill—to know where one is going, how to get there, and how to get back. In fact, your life may depend on it, it is that important. Always there is an innocent tenderfoot who starts out without map or compass and eventually has to be searched for and led back. Orienteering, old in Europe, is growing as a competitive sport in the United States. In Europe it is a cross-country race. It was begun originally as a military training device but now is a highly organized sport with many countries competing in international meets. It is popular in Canada. And it is gradually attracting outdoorsmen, environmentalists, and recreational and athletic enthusiasts in the U.S. It is primarily practiced on foot, but bicyclers, cross-country skiers, and canoers use it, and even those in automobiles. The book by Bengtsson and Atkinson listed below will provide history, techniques, and information for those that would pursue their interest in this sport.

PHYSICAL CONDITIONING.   While extreme old age could be a severe handicap for participation, hiking and backpacking are not activities limited to youth. Bill Merrill, a park ranger with long experience, in his book, The Hiker's & Backpacker's Handbook, tells of people in their 70's and 80's packing along wilderness trails. He also indicates that he has had to help out people, of all ages, who have overexerted. Therefore, the message is clear that anyone planning a backpacking trip should take adequate time for physical conditioning before starting such an adventure. Our daughter and a friend recently backpacked on foot to the bottom of the Grand Canyon. They experienced extreme heat and suffered some from exhaustion. It was only because of their stamina and good physical condition that they were able to make the trip down and back without incident.

Since hiking and backpacking are so dependent on foot and leg power it logically follows that anyone contemplating such an outing should be physically prepared for the trip. Jogging, bicycling, climbing steps carrying a backpack of increased weight each day, all would strengthen leg muscles. Specific exercises are described in books on backpacking, skiing, and cross-country skiing, all of which share the same need for conditioned legs.

ADDITIONAL TIPS FOR OLDER HIKERS AND BACK-PACKERS. The previous pages have covered most of the important tips for older hikers. Reference was made to the importance of good footwear. To increase foot comfort one should have along adequate changes of socks, sometimes 2 pair per day on hard walks where feet may sweat. Keep your feet dry. Since foot power is so vital, one should be alert to incipient skin irritation from walking. Experienced hikers apply moleskin at the slightest sign of chafing. This will protect the sensitive skin from further irritation. Don't wait until blisters form before applying the moleskin. That not only is too late to prevent the irritation, but it also is hazardous later to remove the moleskin from the blistered area.

If you are buying new hiking boots, make certain they fit properly. A sporting goods store can advise on the proper fit. Boots should not be too short so that in descending a steep slope your toes continually jam against the front of the boot. Women often tend to buy boots too small, probably because the boots look large in the first place. Break in your boots well before you start your hiking trip, and don't skimp on quality.

Wear loose-fitting clothing. Don't fall victim to tight jeans that will chafe you as you walk. Layers of clothing that can be removed as the day grows warmer are helpful. Walking shorts are very good on hot days, but be prepared with warm clothing for the evening, especially at high altitudes.

Since hiking, particularly where steep slopes are involved, is fairly strenuous, older people should condition themselves before starting on a long hike. Several shorter hikes can prepare one for the exertion required and will bring out weaknesses in the preparation for the longer outing. Physical preparation should include a check with your doctor to make certain you are in condition to make the hike. Age here is not the only, nor necessarily the most important, consideration. Physical fitness is the controlling factor.

If this is your first time out, pick out a well-marked trail in a national park. Signs will keep you posted on distances to the next campsite. Sign in with the park ranger and tell him about your plan. Start out easy. Stick to the paths. It is perhaps better not to go alone. Keep track of your whereabouts by using maps and your compass. A pair of binoculars can be very useful for viewing the trail ahead, spotting the campsite, and also for studying birds and wildlife which sometimes can best be viewed from a distance. Our daughter Susan recounts her experience of backpacking in the Glacier National Park. She noted a sign which indicated the next campsite as 2.2 miles

ahead. It also was apparent that the trail was a series of switchbacks, indicating a fairly steep grade. She and her friends reached the campsite 6 hours later, in a state of near exhaustion. It, indeed, was a strenuous climb for those 2.2 miles. Studying the trail by means of maps and binoculars can foretell what lies ahead, and helps in the decision to camp or push on to the next campsite.

FOR MORE INFORMATION

There are numerous commercially published books and magazines on hiking and backpacking, which should be available at your public library or local bookstore. Organizations such as the Sierra Club also have compiled useful publications available to members and nonmembers. A few sample titles, illustrating what is available, are listed here as a start.

Books:

Bengtsson, Hans, and George Atkinson. *Orienteering.* Brattleboro, Vt., The Stephen Greene Press, 1977. $5.95.

Colwell, Robert. *Introduction to Foot Trails in America.* New York, Barnes & Noble, 1975. $1.50.

Eggert, Richard. *Backpack Hiking: The First Steps.* Harrisburg, Pa., Stackpole, 1977. $2.95.

Fletcher, Colin. *New Complete Walker.* New York, Knopf, 1974. $10.00.

Kelsey, Robert J. *Walking in the Wild.* New York, Funk & Wagnalls, 1974. $2.50.

Merrill, Bill. *The Hiker's & Backpacker's Handbook.* New York, Arco, 1972. $2.95.

Meves, Eric. *Guide to Backpacking in the United States: Where to Go and How to Get There.* New York, Macmillan, 1978. $3.95.

Roberts, Harry. *Movin' Out: Equipment & Technique for Hikers,* Rev. Ed. Boston, Stone Wall Press, 1979. $4.95.

Rudner, Ruth. *Off and Walking: A Hiker's Guide to American Places.* New York: Holt, Rinehart and Winston, 1977. $4.95.

Sierra Club. Totebooks Series. New York, Scribners.

 Back, Orville. *Hiking the Yellowstone Backcountry.* $5.95.

 Bunnelle, Hasse. *Food for Knapsackers.* $3.95.

 —— with Shirley Sarvis. *Cooking for Camp and Trail.* $3.95.

 Hart, John. *Hiking the Bigfoot Country; the Wildlands of Northern California and Southern Oregon.* $7.95.

 ——. *Walking Softly in the Wilderness: The Sierra Club Guide to Backpacking.* $5.95.

 Lawrance, Paul, *Hiking the Teton Backcountry.* $4.95.

 Murless, Dick, and Constance Stallings. *Hiker's Guide to the Smokies.* $7.95.

 Reifsnyder, William E. *Foot-Loose in the Swiss Alps.* $7.95.

 ——. *Hut Hopping in the Austrian Alps.* $4.95.

 Robinson, Douglas, ed. *Starr's Guide to the John Muir Trail and the High Sierra Region.* $4.95.

 Roper, Steve. *Climber's Guide to Yosemite Valley.* $7.95.

 Rudner, Ruth. *Huts and Hikes in the Dolomites; a Guide to the Trails and Huts of the Italian Alps.* $4.95.

 Van Lear, Denise, ed. *The Best About Backpacking.* $6.95.

Wood, Amos L. *Hiking Trails in the Pacific Northwest.* Matteson, Ill., Greatlakes Living Press, 1977. $5.95.

Magazines:

Appalachian Trailways News. Quarterly. Appalachian Trail Conference, Box 236, Harpers Ferry, W. Va. 25425. $4.00 per year.

Backpacker. Bi-monthly. 65 Adams St., Bedford Hills, N.Y. 10507. $12.00 per year.

Wilderness Camping. Bi-monthly. 1597 Union St., Schenectady, N.Y. 12309. $6.95 per year.

18   *Jogging*

A JOGGING program might be a more effective method of treating abnormal depression than numerous sessions on an analysts's couch," begins a recent news story. It was a report of a psychiatrist's study of a 10-week jogging program undertaken by a small group of patients. While not conclusive, it bears out the claim that there is a positive relationship between exercise and mental health.

Frankly, I find running a bit boring. It is not my favorite form of exercise. I prefer competitive activities where my concentration is on the game, and exercise is a by-product. But there is no denying that jogging elevates the spirit as well as improves the flesh.

Since it requires a fair amount of self-discipline to jog regularly, it is of enormous help if you have some incentive that spurs you on. My wife and I do not jog regularly except for the in-between seasons when other activities are not practical. In the winter we ski and we feel that, if we do it fairly regularly, we keep in condition throughout the ski season—roughly December 15 to March 15. In the late spring, summer, and early fall, we swim, play tennis, water ski, and occasionally golf, again maintaining our physical condition. Where we live in Minnesota, this period lasts from about April 15 to November 1. Of course, one can play tennis indoors if one has access to a school gym or a tennis club. We prefer playing outdoors. Therefore, we resort to jogging for 6 weeks in the late fall and for a month or so in the early spring.

In terms of investment of both time and money, jogging costs very little. A half hour or so daily or several times a week, keeps us in condition. A good pair of athletic shoes and some old loose clothing is all that is required for dress, depending on the climate, of course. Warm-up suits put you in more style, if that is important.

Jogging has not only the attractiveness of low cost but also the great advantage of not requiring any special facilities. Any street, park, sidewalk, field, country road, or woodland path will do. One can run alone, with one's spouse, in a group, or competitively, marking down distances covered in a given time span. There probably is no more versatile sport, nor one that makes less demands on ability or social aptitude. Even your dog can go along for companionship.

Despite these positive assets, jogging still tends to be monotonous. For that reason it is well to give some thought as to ways in which it can be made more fun. For example, measuring the distance you run, and then establishing goals for increasing this within a prescribed time, focuses your interest on competing against your old distance. Choosing an attractive place to jog gets your mind on the scenery and off the tedium of running. One of the most popular jogging places I've observed is along an attractive boulevard beside a river. Not only is the scenery interesting but the very fact that so many others are also there jogging establishes a comradeship with fellow runners and soon you anticipate seeing your trotting, sweaty friends, often passing each other with unspoken greetings.

It should be said that jogging, depending upon the vigor with which you approach it, can be fairly strenuous exercise. Those with any history of cardiac problems, or those beyond 50 years of age, would be well advised to have a physical checkup and consult their physician before undertaking jogging or any other endurance exercise program.

Some advocates of jogging claim one has to run at least 1½ miles to reap benefits from the exercise. At the beginning alternately running and walking is essential so as to build up gradually to the regimen. Some zealots have built up their daily run to 5, 6, or more miles. It must have some attractive aspects!

According to Dr. Kenneth H. Cooper, author of several books on aerobics, you have reached an acceptable degree of physical fitness when you can comfortably run 1½ miles in 12 minutes. To maintain that fitness, you should run it 4 days a week. Others claim that once you have reached an acceptable physical condition, jogging 20 to 30 minutes 3 times a week will do much to maintain it. Dr. Cooper's books are well worth reading, for they provide the guidance necessary to phase in the fitness regimen.

Doctors have their own literature on the pros and cons of jogging, but the cons generally pertain to the degree of strenuous exercise involved, not the fact that such exercise, practiced in appropriate moderation, improves the body and the spirit.

Jogging and running (they overlap in definition) can be addictive. Newspaper accounts tell of a 58-year old man who ran in a marathon race, a distance of just over 26 miles, and did it in under 3 hours. He began running only 4 years earlier, at 54. One runner, an 86-year old grandmother, was reported to have entered the marathon run up and down Pike's Peak in Colorado Springs. Although she didn't complete that race, only a year before she had completed 13 miles of the uphill run. She still regularly jogs and walks 5 miles a day.

The difference between jogging and running is largely a matter of speed and distance. Joggers tend to do a mile in more than 8 minutes; that is, they aren't running against the clock, as are runners. Also, joggers tend to be 1 or 2 milers. Runners will do a mile in less than 8 minutes and think nothing of running 70 to 100 miles in a week. Senator Wendell Anderson, former Governor of Minnesota, runs 5 miles a day in addition to playing hockey regularly in Washington. Runner or jogger? Perhaps most of those over 50 will be content with jogging, although some undoubtedly do become runners as their fitness improves.

Apparently, given proper medical supervision, one hardly becomes too old to jog. In a recent issue of *Woman's Day*, we are given the account of 87-year old Eula Weaver of Santa Monica, California. At 80 she had severe, crippling arthritis, poor blood circulation, and a previous heart attack when she was about 72. One would surmise that the outlook for her future activity was not too bright, to say the least. Her doctor offered her the alternative of being an invalid or getting up and walking around as much as possible. With a controlled, supervised diet and exercise program, beginning with trotting in the park, she began to improve. A year later she was jogging 1½ miles daily and bicycling the equivalent of 15 miles a day on a stationary machine. Now, without pain, she enters footraces for seniors, and wins!

Knowing how to jog is important, especially as one gets older. Experienced joggers prescribe a stride that is comfortable, landing each step on the heel. Landing on the toes will cause back problems and sore legs. It is necessary to have good jogging shoes, those that have an arch support and a thick, spongy heel. Older people, with less give in their frame, can develop difficulties if their body jars sharply with each step. Fortunately, with the high interest today in jogging, footwear manufacturers have developed shoes suitable for jogging. It will pay dividends to invest in good footwear. That is about the only expense to the sport, so $15 or $20 still makes jogging a very low-cost activity.

Because I subscribe to the general proposition that jogging gives beneficial results and can be enjoyable, but at the same time I am not an enthusiastic jogger, you might benefit from reading accounts of more sincere practitioners. There have been numerous magazine articles and newspaper features written on jogging which are available in local public libraries. The published literature is not very large. Most books are written for runners, not joggers, and for athletes, not for those over 50.

The National Jogging Association issues a tabloid newsletter titled *Jogger*, which is very helpful. Membership in the Association ($15) includes 8 issues of *Jogger* annually, special discounts on books on jogging, exercising, and related subjects, and pages of enthusiastic testimony on the value of jogging. The Association was founded in 1968 to boost jogging as the "simplest, cheapest, least encumbered, most available, and most efficient way to achieve physical fitness and build up the heart and lungs."

Many doctors are enthusiastic joggers, runners, and marathoners or endurance runners. There is, in fact, an American Medical Joggers Association, which serves as a common interest forum for discussion and publication on jogging.

If physical fitness becomes an objective of yours, certainly jogging has to be toward the top of the list of activities that will assist in accomplishing that goal. It is well established by medical evidence that jogging is one of the most effective means of conditioning. To recap some of the results of medical experiments, it has been shown that jogging and other exercising can:

1. Reduce high blood pressure
2. Reduce heart rate
3. Reduce fatigue
4. Increase work (or play) capacity
5. Increase pulmonary function
6. Increase circulating blood volume
7. Decrease muscle wasting
8. Decrease obesity
9. Decrease hypertension
10. Lower incidence of coronary heart disease
11. Improve tolerance to emotional stress
12. Reduce depression
13. Improve mental health
14. Improve quality of life
15. Add years to life (and life to years)
16. Slow down the aging process
17. Improve sexual response
18. Aid in rehabilitation of heart attack victims
19. Improve digestion, elimination, and controlled appetite

One hardly needs more justification than such an array of benefits to give jogging a try, even at the risk of being a little bored. It doesn't cost much to find out whether you like it. But don't expect miracles the first week. Experts claim it may take up to 4 weeks of regular participation to begin noticing improvements in your condition.

TIPS FOR OLDER JOGGERS.   A young woman colleague of mine recently told me that she gave up jogging because she had developed shin splints, that is, very sore and painful shins. I strongly suspect that she had been running and landing on the ball of her foot or her toes rather than on her heel. This is an important bit of technique for everyone who jogs, but it becomes increasingly important as one gets older. Some advocates say that jogging should be more of a glide than a run, so that one does not jar the spine so hard with each step. Land flat on your feet or on your heel. Once you start to jog you will experiment with different strides and you will find the one most comfortable and least tiring for you. Don't try for distance.

My wife and I find that by taking easy, soft steps, not fast, large strides, we have surprising endurance.

One of the least understood aspects of exercises such as jogging is the important role that proper diet plays. Interviews with the 1976 Olympic athletes revealed they had little understanding of the value, for example, of honey and high-protein foods for building strength and endurance. Sugar taken before exercising, contrary to popular belief, actually reduces endurance because of the effect it has on the insulin content of the body and the sugar in the blood. According to some tests, eating sugar 30 to 40 minutes before exercising can reduce endurance as much as 19 percent. The best preparation for strenuous exercising, such as marathon running, appears to be a diet high in complex carbohydrates, such as fruits, vegetables, and breads. For joggers, apparently a well-balanced diet, little alcohol, and, of course, no smoking, should serve to keep us in the running regardless of our age.

Fun and fitness has been the underlying message throughout this book. What you do should be enjoyable. There is a Catch-22 here, of course, and I can think of no better place to discuss it than when we are talking about jogging. Joe Henderson, editor of *Runner's World*, said it best in a recent issue of *Wilderness Camping*. He said, "Fun and fitness go together. . . . You can't enjoy that lovely canoe trip at Quetico when your lungs are bursting with the effort of breathing. Cross-country skiing when you're gasping like a carp out of water just isn't cross-country skiing. It simply isn't fun—and fun is why you're there in the first place. You can't have fun until you're reasonably fit. And you can't stay fit unless you're having fun at it. The two feed on each other: they grow from a program of regular, gently-paced running."

One of the problems older people have in jogging is self-discipline. There are so many alleged excuses one can find for not running. It may be tiredness, social engagements, not enough time, not wanting to delay dinner, and on and on. It is a fact that people do what they most want to do, and find excuses for not doing things they don't want to do. Recognizing that trait in all of us, we respond more regularly if we make commitments. Neighbors of ours run early each morning, together. So far only the wives seem to be out. They admit that the reason several run together is that they make a commitment to each other and they want to live up to it. If they hadn't done it that way, each would often find reasons for not getting up so early and jogging. A man and wife can do that just as well. I know, for often it is my wife who is instrumental in our going jogging. A suggestion from someone else appears to be enough to tip the balance in favor of going rather than staying in.

There is an addiction to running, according to testimony from numerous joggers. Some may get started to improve their fitness. Often, after the initial period of concentrating on fitness is over, comes a realization that there is more to jogging than fitness. There is an exhilaration, an enjoyment of the jogging itself as an activity. Ultimately some reach a philosophical involvement similar to meditation. Some find jogging stimulates the mind, helps in problem solving, results in creative thinking, and elevates the spirit to a new level. A few claim to get a high from jogging similar to that induced by some drugs. However euphoric it becomes probably depends on what one brings to jogging at the start. A flabby, smoking and drinking, sedentary type who takes up jogging will after several months feel like a different person, I'll bet, and that's enough to make a meditator out of anyone. Be advised, therefore, that this activity, if pursued regularly, may be good for your health.

FOR MORE INFORMATION

The Sunday supplements and slick magazines are strewn with articles about jogging. There also are an increasing number of books, some of which have become best sellers, attesting to jogging's popularity. Following is a sample of some that are available. Check your library or bookstore for other titles.

Books:

Batten, Jack. *The Complete Jogger.* New York, Harcourt Brace Jovanovich, 1977. $4.95.

Fixx, James. *The Complete Book of Running.* New York, Random, 1977. $10.00.
One of the newest and best books on running and jogging.

Gilmore, Hayden. *Jog for Your Life.* New Ed. Grand Rapids, Mi., Zondervan, 1974. $1.50.
Excessively wordy but enthusiastic testimony to the value of jogging. More inspiration than guidance for the beginning jogger.

Harris, W. E. *Jogging: A Complete Physical Fitness Program for All Ages.* New York, Grosset & Dunlap, 1967. $1.95.
An introduction to jogging with programs for those now inactive, for those in average condition, and for the more active.

Kostrubala, Thaddeus. *Joy of Running.* Philadelphia, Lippincott, 1976. $3.95.
Explains why running works, how to do it, how to determine safe running pace. A psychologist's prescription for leading a longer, better life, whatever your age. Interesting section on jogging and its relation to mind and body.

Roby, Frederick B. J., and Russell P. Davis. *Jogging for Fitness & Weight Control.* Philadelphia, Pa., Saunders, 1970. $3.00.
An excellent introduction to jogging, with self-testing program.

Ullyot, Joan. *Women's Running.* Mountain View, Ca., World Publications, 1976. $3.95.
Admitting to hating exercise she *loves* running because it is exhilarating, providing the euphoria of living to one's full capacity. Health benefits are a peripheral bonus.

Magazines:

Jogger. 8 times a year. National Jogging Association, 1910 K Street, Washington, D.C. 20006. Membership $15 per year.

19 *Cross-Country Skiing*

FEW SPORTS have enjoyed a quicker rise in popularity than cross-country skiing, or ski-touring, as some call it. Various explanations have been given for the increased interest in this winter sport. One obvious attraction is its low cost. It also appeals to a wide range of age groups, from 6 to 90 years. And, perhaps above all, it is a sport that enables the skier to reach remote, isolated areas in winter to observe nature wearing its most glorious mantle.

Cross-country skiing received a major boost as a popular sport in the U.S. when 1976 Olympic Games viewers watched Bill Koch, of Vermont, capture the silver medal in the 30-kilometer race. It was the first time the U.S. had won a medal in this sport. It was an inspiring performance and undoubtedly spurred many to try it for themselves.

One of the memorable cross-country skiing experiences we had recently took us high in the mountains of Colorado, away from nearly all signs of civilization. It was one of those perfect unmatched days with brilliant sunshine, azure blue skies, and glistening white snow. The temperature in the early morning was a crisp 15° F. There was no wind. We gathered at 8 a.m. with our guide. He saw that each of us in the group of 12 was properly outfitted. It took about an hour of preparation. We divided the packs among us, checking provisions, and getting the proper wax on our skis. We boarded our several cars and headed for Berthoud Pass. Arriving near the 10,000-foot elevation, we abandoned the cars and mounted our skis. For the next 2½ hours we zigzagged up the mountain to about 11,000 feet. We stopped frequently to catch our breath and to inhale the beauty that only a poet could adequately describe.

Our guide this day was a young, trim college boy who obviously was an expert. He set the trail and advised on the correct wax to use as the temperature increased. He was as ecstatic as the rest of us with the beautiful scenery. Frequently he took quick side excursions to capture a particularly beautiful vista with his camera.

At that elevation the air is rare and we needed to rest more frequently as we climbed upward. Also, with bright sun and no wind, the exertion of climbing forced everyone in the group to continuously shed clothing, until, at the point of reaching our destination about noon, most of us were in shirtsleeves, and even then perspiring. One secret of dressing for such an outing is to wear several layers of jackets and sweaters so that these can be peeled off or put back on as the situation requires.

Our destination was a very small, crude abandoned cabin about half way to the summit of the mountain. Once there we doffed our skis and excess clothing and basked in the delicious sunshine that can only be found high in the mountains. After a simple trail lunch most of us put on our skis again and roamed around the area, observing the nearby glacier. A young couple, with their dogs romping in the snow, were skiing a nearby slope, forming a beautiful alpine view for us.

The indescribable beauty of that mountainscape, the absolute quiet, and the exhilaration of the exercise and companionship of the morning, will live in our minds forever. Except for the guide, who was the youngest person in the party, our group ranged in age from the 30's to mid-60's. Those of us at the upper end of the range appeared to have less exhaustion than the younger ones. Perhaps we have learned to pace ourselves better. But this outing was added evidence for me to believe that cross-country skiing is a sport for all ages.

At first one might assume that climbing upward 1000 feet on skis, on a warm day, at very high altitude, would be a very exhausting experience. To be sure, by the time we reached our stopping place, it felt good to relax. But we certainly didn't feel like collapsing. In fact almost all of us kept walking around, exploring the rocks and terrain nearby. Surprisingly, the more exhausting experience was the return trip down the mountain. Unlike alpine skis, cross-country skis offer the skier very little control in either speed or direction. An experienced skier no doubt could descend a gentle slope by making very large S-curves. Generally, however, with cross-country skis one establishes the direction and then proceeds more or less in a straight line. All the more reason that the direction chosen is over a slope that is gentle, with just enough drop to move the skier forward in a glide but not so steep that he loses control. This is the responsibility of the guide who sets the trail and all in the party follow in his tracks.

Descending 1000 feet on cross-country skis is likely to require a couple of hours, unlike alpine skiing, which may require only a few minutes. It is necessary to zigzag back and forth, continuously maintaining the trail on a very gentle descent. Occasionally, as one reaches the point of changing direction, there is no choice but to deliberately sit or fall down in the snow if the trail hasn't been properly chosen to break the speed at the right place. Once you are down in the deep powder snow, it requires a special effort to right yourself. After you struggle to your feet, brush the snow off, clean your glasses (and sunglasses or goggles, which are an absolute essential in mountain skiing), and get properly oriented in the ski trail again, you're somewhat breathless. By the time you experience that kind of activity a few times, you begin to understand that coming back down the mountain sometimes can be more exhausting than climbing it.

CROSS-COUNTRY SKIING VS. ALPINE SKIING. In alpine skiing, the skis are about 5 feet long, depending upon the skier's height, perhaps 4 inches wide, and have bindings that rigidly clamp heavy boots onto the skis so that any foot movement will be transmitted to the ski. Cross-country skis, on the other hand, are very lightweight, long and narrow, and the bindings clasp almost featherlight oxford-type boots only at the toe with a hinged tension grip. Once mounted the skier has a freedom of movement quite unlike the alpine skier. In alpine skiing, the skier can maneuver the skis to control both speed and direction, whereas the cross-country skier generally propels himself forward in a walking–gliding motion. The alpine skier basically depends upon a fairly steep slope and the force of gravity to move him forward. The cross-country skier seeks out level or gentle slopes, in woods and fields or golf courses, or occasionally, as on the outing described, even climbs mountains with his skis. Whereas both kinds of skiing depend upon snow and skis, they are in many respects two different sports, and have their own advocates. Often, of course, participants in one will also enjoy the other, but it would be a mistake to think of them in one category.

What about age differences among the participants? I have heard some say, "I'm too old for downhill skiing so I go cross-country skiing." Our experience is that it requires more exertion, and in some respects even is more hazardous, to cross-country ski than to downhill ski. There are downhill skiers as well as cross-country skiers in their 70's and 80's.

One major advantage of cross-country skiing is that without a large expenditure of either time or money, you can find an open field or golf course or park, put on your skis and in an hour or so, complete your outing, having had good exercise and an enjoyable, virtually cost-free experience. So many sports, alpine skiing included, require a half day or more to participate fully, and often at considerable expense. Another plus for cross-country skiing is that any good snow cover will open the opportunity for skiing. Snow conditions, temperature, and weather are less critical than for alpine skiing. With the proper choice of wax, one can adjust to variable conditions, and happily glide across the snow-covered terrain, enjoying the beauty and peace of remote areas abandoned by all others except the animals and winter birds.

COSTS AND CHARACTERISTICS OF CROSS–COUNTRY SKIS. Waxing the skis is a big thing in cross-country skiing, as we most certainly discovered as we worked our way up the Colorado mountain. Special waxes have been developed that, paradoxically, will let you glide forward but will resist slipping backward. This is not the place to explain this phenomenon (fortunately!), but be assured that as snow conditions and temperatures change, it becomes necessary to change the wax. Say you start skiing in the early

Cross-country skier executes a simple step turn.

morning. Temperatures probably are well below freezing. The snow is made up of frozen particles created by the cold night that followed yesterday's warmth. Later in the day the bright sunshine softens the snow to the point at which it is beginning to melt. During the day, then, you have two very different surfaces upon which you are gliding. These two extremes require two quite different waxes. With one exception, there is no avoiding the mastering of the art of waxing if you are going to be a participant in cross-country skiing.

The exception to the need for waxing, mostly shunned and perhaps even scoffed at by the aficionado, is to buy skis that have a fish-scale bottom surface. This will permit forward motion but impede the backward slide. There are continuous developments of such surfaces and if you don't want to have the "fun" (some would read "bother") of waxing, you might do well to consider such skis. They probably will cost more but the advantage to you may be worth it.

Without a doubt one of the attractive features of cross-country skiing is its relatively low cost. It is possible to get outfitted with equipment and boots for under $100. Most ski shops offer package bargains—skis, bindings, poles, and boots—the essentials for you to begin. Clothing can be from your own closet or trunk. It is essential that you obtain several different waxes to be used on varying snow conditions. Dark glasses are advisable because of the glare of the snow, especially if you are in high altitudes, where sun damage to the eyes can come quickly and painfully. Also some skin protection against the sun in mountainous areas is recommended.

Skis are long, narrow, and made of wood. The base, also of natural wood, requires a protective tar coat to prevent excessive wear and also to serve as a proper base for the wax. Poles are long and lightweight, often made of aluminum or bamboo. The boots or shoes worn depend on the kind of binding used. The pin-type binding grasps the front of the sole of the boot, which has holes in it that match the pins. Cable bindings, on the other hand, permit the use of other footwear. With these you can, if you wish, ski in your overshoes, hiking or work boots, or shoes. The bindings all permit your heel to move freely up and down as you propel yourself forward in a walk–glide motion. The poles assist you in balancing, in pushing yourself forward, and in preventing your sliding backward when going up a slope.

Like many sports, cross-country skiing can be most enjoyed if you learn the basics from a qualified or at least knowledgeable instructor. It may make the difference between discouragement and pleasure, exhaustion and invigoration. Unlike many sports, one can achieve a level of mastery of cross-country skiing in a relatively short time—perhaps even a half day—giving one the feeling of fast becoming an expert.

PHYSICAL REQUIREMENTS. A question that needs to be addressed is: How strenuous a sport is cross-country skiing? How does one get physically prepared? As one writer states it, "If you can walk, you can ski." While that is reassuring, the fact is that cross-country skiing is exhausting at first and quite easy after you have learned the technique. All the more reason to learn the "how to" as quickly as possible.

Naturally, it is essential that you be in condition for moderately strenuous exercise before you go very far on skis. Your doctor ought to advise you as to whether it is appropriate for you to ski. Leg muscles and arm and shoulder muscles will tire and ache in reverse proportion to your physical condition. The better shape you're in, the less likely you will be to have sore muscles. Doing conditioning exercises for a couple of weeks before skiing will pay off in the enjoyment of your experience on skis.

WHERE TO SKI. With the increased popularity of cross-country skiing, many more agencies are providing places to ski. In urban areas, parks departments have opened city and county parks to skiing and often provide a program for maintenance of ski trails. Public golf courses and recreation areas often have ski trails or permit skiers to roam over the hills on their own. Check with the U.S. Forest Service for permission to use the wooded areas under their jurisdiction.

Information on ski trails can often be obtained from state departments of natural resources, parks, tourism, or recreation. Also there are city and county agencies which control the recreation areas within their jurisdictions. Golf course managers can advise on the availability of their facilities. If you own a lakeshore cottage or have a friend who does, cross-country skiing can give an entirely different perspective on, and new enjoyment of, familiar territory.

Because of the popularity of cross-country skiing, many ski resorts that formerly limited their activity to alpine skiing, have developed ski trails and provide guides. This has furthered the interest in cross-country skiing among alpine skiers who are interested in seeing remote parts of mountains and exploring beautiful mountain streams and meadows previously ignored or unreachable. Some guests at such resorts are there only for cross-country skiing and enjoy the benefits and pleasures of après-skiing as much as alpine skiers.

TIPS FOR OLDER CROSS–COUNTRY SKIERS. A popular misconception, even among skiers themselves, is that cross-country skiing requires little physical exertion. Experts make it appear

A cross-country skier demonstrates excellent form. His weight shifts forward as he springs ahead from the back ski. This active "sprint" requires no extra warm clothing. In fact, if he gets overheated, the skier can remove his wool cap.

effortless, but like all sports cross-country skiing has few experts. Therefore I willingly lay myself on the line and say that cross-country skiing is a rather strenuous activity, especially if done competitively, and is pretty hard work if one skis anything other than flat surfaces, such as frozen lakes. In Chapter 2 I presented charts showing degrees of energy required for different sports. Slow cross-country skiing (2.5 mph) in loose snow is shown to be equivalent to vigorous basketball or running 5.5 mph. Obviously, one should be in reasonably good physical condition to take up serious cross-country skiing.

Dressing appropriately is an essential element in enjoyable cross-country skiing. It is very easy to overdress because often the ski touring outing begins at the time of day when the air is nippy and crisp.

Of course, one must keep comfortable during this period, so dressing warmly is important. Inevitably, however, even on cold days, the body begins to react to the physical exertion soon after one starts skiing, and it is necessary to adjust the amount of clothing worn. The secret is to wear layers of outer clothing that can easily be removed and carried. Most cross-country skiers carry a knapsack for such clothing along with the necessary waxes, scrapers, and other items that may be needed.

If you plan to head into the back country or over a mountain pass, you would do well to carry an extra ski tip with you. It is not uncommon to break your ski at the tip, and if you should do so without an emergency tip to tide you over, you could be in rather dire straits if you have to work your way out of deep snow for any distance. An older skier in such a situation may overextend himself, with the chances of serious consequences. It quite possibly could be a matter of life or death to heed this suggestion, especially if you are skiing alone.

The temptation to cross-country ski is greatest on a bright winter day, with brilliant sunshine and glistening snow. By all means prepare for the glare and sunburn you will experience. Sunglasses are essential at the very least. If the outing is to be an extended one, lasting several hours or more, a blocking cream will prevent sunburn. This advice is especially pertinent if one is skiing at high altitudes where the effects of the bright snow are much greater than they are in wooded lowlands.

One of the great attractions of cross-country skiing is that it enables one to travel to remote places normally visited only by wild animals and a few birds. Unless you are continually alert as to where you are and where your starting point is, it is very easy to get hopelessly lost. This can be quite serious, especially on cold days and particularly if it should start snowing while you are back in the woods. To guard against the panic that inevitably is experienced on getting lost, carry a good compass. Also practice the buddy system so that there will be more than one person to cope with any emergency situation. A few provisions in the knapsack may be useful to maintain your energy, should that be necessary. Also you might want to acquaint yourself with the techniques of orienteering, mentioned in Chapter 17.

FOR MORE INFORMATION

If you don't mind the cold and snow, if you enjoy wintry beauty and want to see it at its best, and want to join thousands who are enjoying an invigorating sport, you ought to try cross-country skiing. Here are a few books and magazines that will give you the information you need to get started. These and others should be available at your public library or bookstore, and at some sporting goods stores.

Books:

Bauer, Erwin A. *Cross-country Skiing and Snowshoeing.* South Hackensack, N.J., Stoeger, 1976. $5.95.

Written by an outdoor writer/photographer, this book lauds the quietness and peacefulness of the winter wonderland enjoyed only by those on skis and snowshoes. Well illustrated, this is a useful, inspiring why and where guide rather than a how-to.

Brady, M. Michael, and Lorns O. Skjemstad. *Ski Cross-Country.* New York, Dial, 1974. $5.95.

Originally published in Norway, the home of cross-country skiing. This is a handbook of fundamentals that are essential for the beginner. The many illustrations make this guide easy to use for beginners and experienced skiers, for the tourer and the racer.

Caldwell, John. *Cross-Country Skiing Today.* Brattleboro, Vt., The Stephen Greene Press, 1977. $4.95.

Good as a guide, especially on details of waxing, group racing, and exercises in preparation for skiing.

Editors of *Nordic World. Discover Cross-Country Skiing.* Mountain View, Ca., World Publications, 1974. $1.50.

A brief, handy, and inexpensive handbook; very useful, with good illustrations.

——. *Nordic Skiing Gear.* Mountain View, Ca., World Publications, 1974. $1.75.

Companion volume to the one above. Focuses on equipment, with tables of available skis, boots, manufacturers. Dated.

Freeman, Cortlandt L. *Steve Rieschl's Ski-Touring for the Fun of It.* Boston, Little, Brown, 1974. $3.95.

An excellent beginner's guide with numerous illustrations on technique.

Lund, Morten. *The Pleasures of Cross-Country Skiing.* New York, Avon, 1972. $2.95.

Useful beginner's guide, well illustrated.

Tapley, Lance. *Ski Touring in New England and New York; A Complete Cross-Country Ski Book.* Rev. Ed. Boston, Stone Wall Press, 1976. $4.95.

Guide to the basics of equipment and technique. Also includes an extensive guide to touring places in New England and New York.

Tejada-Flores, Lito, and Allen Steck. *Wilderness Skiing.* A Sierra Club Totebook. New York, Scribners. $6.95.

Magazines:

Nordic World. Monthly, September to March. World Publication, P.O. Box 366, Mountain View, Ca. 94042. $6.50 per year.

20 *Downhill Skiing*

PROBABLY the biggest bores at a cocktail party are the downhill skiers. They seem to want to talk of nothing else but skiing. Not about their prowess, not boasting about the posh resorts they've skied—their talk is sheer enthusiasm for the sport of skiing. We were non-skiers at just such a party several years ago and fell under the spell of an enthusiastic couple who had recently returned from a week of skiing at Winter Park, Colorado.

Several weeks later, with considerable trepidation, my wife and I decided to venture out to a local ski slope, rent some equipment, and take a skiing lesson. We were both in our mid-50's, and were still quite agile. Prior to this occasion, when we had taken one of our children to a local ski slope, we had observed that many of those skiing were no more athletic than we, and some were nearly our age. We remarked, "If they can do it, why can't we?"

The decision for us to try skiing took courage, to say the least, especially at our age. But that day was one of our most memorable experiences. We came home exhausted but absolutely exhilarated. Skiing literally has changed our lives, certainly our attitudes. Winter had become for us something of a drag. Now we "think snow" and lament the passing of the skiing season.

That first experience on skis began as if it were going to be a nightmare. We arrived at the ski chalet for the lesson in what seemed to be ample time. But the fitting of the rented boots and bindings took longer than we expected. We finally emerged from the equipment room, trying to move forward on the most awkward footwear imaginable, and long skis that didn't want to track. We inquired as to the whereabouts of the instructor. We were told that he already had taken his class to the top of the hill. Aghast, we had no choice but to join them up there. And the only way to get there was on skis! With crossed fingers and pounding pulse we glided, happily without incident, down a gentle slope to the rope tow. We had not the faintest idea how that contraption worked. Skiers are very helpful to other skiers, so we were instructed where to stand, how to grab the rope, and how to be propelled up the hill. We did it! That was the beginning for us of pure adventure for the winters that followed.

What, you might ask, is so great about skiing that it has attracted an estimated 6 million people here in the U.S. alone? Above all skiing gives one an almost overwhelming feeling of accomplishment. That feeling predominates from the very first day. But that by no means is the only thing that generates such enthusiasm for the sport. Typically one is surrounded by happy people enjoying themselves, almost silently. There is no sport I know of, except skiing, where hundreds of participants are involved and about the only sounds you hear are the skis swishing against the snow. Even on the chair lifts skiers talk in muffled tones as if not to disturb the silence and beauty of the nature around them. A ride up a long mountain lift that takes you through snow-covered pine trees and offers you breathtaking views of scenery many miles around, with silent skiers below you cascading down the mountainside, is an unforgettable experience.

There is something else that skiing offers that brings you back to the slopes. You are pitted against yourself in a challenge that never ceases. Something compels you to improve your skiing ability, to try a slope a bit more difficult, to explore new areas you haven't skied before. You experience a new thrill in having negotiated a mogul that yesterday seemed too difficult for you.

Not all days are supremely happy, of course. Some are downright discouraging because you skied worse than ever, you didn't meet your expectations, and you fell a few times and it frightened you. Yes, you fell! What about all this talk of the dangers of skiing? Would you believe that we have skied among thousands of skiers, for days, and only occasionally have we seen injuries severe enough for the ski patrol to become involved? Of course, there are accidents and injuries, as there are in any activity, including walking. The truth is that the design of skiing equipment has progressed to the point that serious accidents are the exception, not the rule. The fear of injuries is no longer a valid reason for not skiing.

Today it can be said truthfully that skiing is a relatively safe sport. Of course, there are risks, and sometimes the safety of new equipment is overly touted. But risk-taking is a natural part of our technological age. As someone once said, the only hazard-free area in this world is the graveyard. There are always trade-offs—more cars, more accidents; higher speeds, more fatalities. We have become somewhat immune to the dangers of everyday living. More of my friends have hurt themselves slipping on sidewalks than from skiing. If one consciously engages in a sport that has some risks involved, one tends to focus, too much perhaps, on those risks. On the other hand, if one lived in such a way as always to avoid risks, life would be very boring. As John Auran, in his book *The Ski Better Book*, states:

> Skiing is risky but not unsafe. Researchers in preventive medicine are finding that calculated risk-taking is part of human nature and a healthy exercise both mentally and physically. Taking a calculated risk and succeeding is a stimulating and occasionally euphoric experience. That is why skiing, with its risks, is such a satisfying sport.

The instructor is teaching the class to keep their weight forward, on top of their skis, with their shoulders continually parallel to the slope. This allows one to ski under control and turn easily.

It is important to reduce the risks, he advises, by combining technical skill, good equipment, and experience.

Skiing at 55! Or worse, *starting* to ski at 55! That certainly crossed our minds our first time out. Later in that first year of our skiing we made reservations at a Colorado ski lodge. We mused that we probably would feel somewhat out of place among all the youngsters and that we might be a bit of a curiosity. To our great surprise, when we arrived we found that not only were we very much at home in the lodge among other folks our age and older, but we were by no means the only older couple new to skiing. One old gentleman, at age 75, was still having the time of his life on the slopes. Jean-Claude Killy, one of the world's greatest skiers, in his book *133 Skiing Lessons*, says he knows many ski instructors who have given 70-year old students their first lessons.

Age, the enemy of many sports, has not conquered skiers. Unfortunately, it has overcome many who have not skied and are afraid to try it. That is profoundly regrettable. Lowell Thomas is still skiing at 84 years of age! One grand old lady we met in Colorado, reputedly about 90, had just recently given up downhill and was limiting herself to cross-country skiing! Dr. Merritt Stiles, co-author of *Ski at Any Age*, skis 2 days per week, if possible. He's 75. When skiing season is over, he jogs 2 miles, 3 or more times each week. He claims to be in infinitely better health, at 75, than he was at 55. Too old, you think, to have a try at one of the greatest adventures in sports? I doubt it.

So what does one do to get started, you ask? What's involved? How much will it cost? How do I learn? Where do I go? What do I need to do to become physically prepared? There are books on skiing, of course, and several good magazines. Some of these are listed at the end of this chapter. I'll only give you some general answers here to provide enough information to help you determine if skiing is for you.

EQUIPMENT SELECTION AND COSTS. Downhill skiing, sometimes called alpine skiing, is a moderately expensive sport. If you're the kind that doesn't mind going out occasionally for a steak dinner, there's no problem. On the other hand, if your budget is limited pretty much to Social Security income, there might be better alternatives for getting your physical activity, such as cross-country skiing.

Equipment costs are generally one-time expenses, unless you feel that you have to have the latest styles in clothing and equipment. Few sports place more emphasis on new designs than skiing. Each year there are alleged improvements in boots, bindings, skis, goggles, clothing, gloves, and even ski poles.

Certainly at the start you may want to rent equipment several times. You will know soon after you try skiing whether it really is for you. Then, too, a little experience with rental equipment will help to acquaint you with details that may determine what kind of equipment best suits you.

Among the more expensive parts of your equipment are your boots. Like other commodities, they come in various price ranges. Moderately priced boots will cost up to $100 a pair. Some of the touted brands, and probably better quality, may run to $150 or more. We rented boots our first season and then took advantage of season-end discounts, where 20 to 40 percent reductions are common. Don't buy second-hand boots any more than you would buy used shoes. Proper fitting boots are absolutely essential not only for comfort but, even more importantly, for proper control of your skis. Probably the most important investment you will make, with respect to equipment, is in your boots.

In recent years there has been a major change in skis. Today's skis are durable, mostly fiber glass, and generally no longer need waxing except under certain circumstances. Also, skis are much shorter than they used to be, making skiing for beginners easier. Prices for skis, with bindings, will vary considerably, but a good, new pair will cost $100 or more. Used skis will cost less, of course, and may be adequate if properly selected. In either case, whether you buy new or used skis, invest in new, good-quality bindings. They are not that expensive and are important for protection against injury.

I certainly would recommend purchasing boots, skis, and bindings through a reputable sports shop. Ask plenty of questions. Ski shop personnel are friendly and helpful, and seldom have we experienced bad advice or high-pressure salesmanship.

As to clothes, these can be incidental or expensive—it all depends on your taste. Many young skiers favor blue jeans and sweaters over expensive designer clothes. Chances are that you will want to invest in a good ski jacket that may cost $50 or more. The main consideration is that you have comfortable, warm clothes. To some extent where you ski will determine the kinds of clothes you will want to get. If you ski in Minnesota, warmth is the prime consideration. If you go to posh resorts, style may be an important factor in your selection. Work into your ski togs gradually and don't let the cost of stylish clothes keep you from enjoying the sport.

PHYSICAL PREPARATION.   Most sports require the participants to prepare physically through general or special exercises. This is especially true of skiing. Toning up leg muscles is probably the most important part of physical training. Control of your skis will depend upon legs that won't become tired too soon. There is a reason

Advanced skiers head down a steep slope. The skier second from the front is perfectly and comfortably positioned on top of his skis, perpendicular to the slope. All the skiers are properly poling in front for better edge control of their skis and better balance. The skier in white is "checking" his forward speed as he turns back into the mountain while preparing for his next turn.

why the highest percentage of skiing injuries occurs in the afternoon shortly before the day ends—on "the last run." You may not feel the tiredness, but you may notice that you have less control of your skis. When that happens, head for the chalet and call it a day.

Strengthening and conditioning arm and shoulder muscles also is important. Your safety doesn't depend as much on this, however. Mainly you are going to be using these muscles as you pole down the slope and especially as you approach the ski lift. Unless you don't mind waking up with stiff, sore shoulders, a few regular conditioning exercises several weeks prior to your ski outing is essential.

WHERE TO GO.   Except for the deep south, there are ski slopes all over the United States. Naturally, the best skiing is where there is consistent cold throughout the winter. We feel that the world's best skiing is in Colorado, but that statement may be challenged by Utah, Montana, Vermont, and many other states, each with justification. California, Washington, Oregon, Arizona, North Carolina, and other places normally considered "warm" states, also have good skiing in mountain areas.

To start, you don't need very much by way of hills or fancy lifts. A small mound with a rope tow is enough to provide the beginner with a place to take lessons. And that leads me to one of the absolute requirements: Start skiing with lessons! It will be your wisest investment in this sport. Fundamentals can be learned much faster, and, most important, you will have an understanding of those factors that contribute to your safety. Check the adult education offerings where you live. Chances are that there are classes in skiing given, at very nominal costs.

Once you learn the fundamentals and have practiced on small slopes in your vicinity, try the mountains for real thrills and lots of practice. If you don't live near mountain ski areas, there probably are ski clubs in your city that you can join. These clubs travel in groups, at reduced rates, on skiing outings. Also, many airlines have ski-week packages through which you can make arrangements for special rates that include transportation, lodging, and lift tickets. You can go on your own equally easily if you want to drive. Generally, it is wise to make advance reservations at resorts or lodges. Often motels in the vicinity of a mountain are available unless it happens to be the Christmas or spring break, when many students will be skiing. Those are times to avoid anyhow, since lift lines tend to be long and you get less skiing per hour when you have to spend 10 or 15 minutes at the lift each time you want to go up the hill.

TIPS FOR SKIERS OVER 50.   Among the activities discussed in this book, none is likely to create more apprehensions than downhill skiing, primarily because of the presumed danger involved. With adequate preparation and precautions, one can minimize these alleged dangers so that skiing may be less hazardous than the drive to and from the ski slope.

To engage in any moderately strenuous physical activity, it is only common sense first to achieve more than a minimal level of fitness. I touched on this above in the section on physical preparation. For weeks before the start of the ski season, it is essential to engage in such exercises as skipping rope, jogging, climbing stairs, or a number of other exercises designed particularly for skiers. A good book on skiing will be helpful in choosing these. Leg muscles that do not tire too easily will be a critical factor in your ability to ski and control your skis, thus protecting yourself against many of the risks of skiing.

Assuming, then, that you are physically in shape for skiing, there are a number of things you can do to increase your enjoyment and reduce the chances of injury. One of the greatest handicaps to the older skier is the fear of falling down, with the expected consequence of injury. As soon as possible one must learn to ski in a relaxed attitude. The first few times down a slope when I begin a new ski season I find my legs and feet almost painfully tired. What I'm doing, of course, is skiing under tension and it is not until I feel I have control of my skis that I begin to relax. Soon I am skiing much better and, of course, enjoying it more. One of the keys to reducing tension is to start out on slopes that are easily within your capability. Gentle, wide "meadows" will provide an opportunity for you to get your ski-legs, and then you are on your way.

Once you have relaxed and are in control of your skis, choose slopes that are within your skiing range. Naturally you will seek out new runs and challenges, but it is especially important for the older skier not to get over his head on a slope that is too advanced. This is sure to induce fear, and a chain reaction seems to set in. One tenses up and loses control, with the possible result of a nasty fall and even an injury. Even worse, perhaps, the skier may get discouraged and ultimately develop a dislike for skiing. There is no justification for this turn of events. Keep to the slopes within your ability class and soon you will safely graduate to the next class or to some of the more difficult runs within your class. Overcoming fear should be the first major objective of the older skier.

It is to be expected that while skiing you are going to be surrounded by younger skiers. Some will be quite young. Soon you will encounter the "hot dog" skier—usually a small youngster who starts at the top of the slope and heads straight down the fall line, often at great speeds. Woe to the person who gets in his way, for often these hot-doggers are skiing out of control and cannot maneuver around skiers in their path. It behooves one to keep a wary eye out for these and other skiers who may be approaching from behind. My only near injuries in the years I have been skiing have been the times I tangled with a hot-dog.

Choosing the right snow conditions is especially important for senior skiers. One of my most frustrating and exhausting experiences was when we arrived early on the slope the morning after a beautiful overnight mountain snowfall. The scenery as we ascended the lift was breathtaking. Only a few skiers had been out and, of course, the snow maintenance equipment had not yet started dressing the slopes.

It was a great opportunity, we thought, to experience the much-touted powder snow. For a few minutes we had the surrealistic experience of floating amidst the snow as we began our descent. But we weren't experienced in skiing powder snow. This, we quickly learned, requires the reverse of almost all our previously learned techniques. Inevitably we landed, face down, in 18 inches of feather-like snow! It took us the better part of a half hour to reassemble, de-snow, and struggle out to a path made by a few other earlier skiers for the rest of the descent. It is an exhausting way to begin a day. That is not to say that skiing powder isn't fun. It obviously is. But don't try it until you know how.

Other snow conditions to be alert to occur the morning after a warm day, especially on slopes that face the south or west. There the snow will have softened, even melted, the day before, and during the cold night icy, treacherous patches will develop here and there. Better to wait until the sun softens these slopes before tackling them. They are hazardous, and hitting ice unsuspectingly can be a frightening experience. By tacking slowly back and forth down such slopes one can negotiate them, but that isn't much fun.

Since endurance diminishes as one gets older, one must adjust the day's skiing to maintain the proper energy level. A short chalet break every hour or so, and a rest at noon, enjoying the alpine sun, will help keep a physically fit person in shape to ski all day. The important consideration is to stop skiing when you get tired. You will lose the necessary tight control of your skis if you don't, and control is the secret to safe skiing. To counter tiredness, it is well to remember that a light lunch is better than a heavy one, coffee is better than alcohol, and a cool place is preferable to an overheated one while taking your rest breaks.

Those unaccustomed to being outdoors on a bright sunny winter day often do not realize that they are exposed doubly to the effects of the sun, both from direct and from reflected rays. It is especially critical in mountain skiing that one use a blocking cream to protect oneself against overexposure. Younger skiers, of course, are seeking sun tans, but I have seen painful blisters, especially around the mouth, on older people who have not adequately guarded against the bright mountain sun. Apparently, according to doctors, such rays promote a certain virus which is very difficult to treat and quick relief is not likely for a few days.

Sun, of course, is a great ally of the skier in other ways. On sunny days the moguls and other irregular terrain can be clearly seen. This is essential, especially for older skiers. In fact, my wife and I choose the days we ski on the basis of whether or not the sun is shining. It is a bit frightening to ski on slopes which are not familiar to you on days when there is no sun. Often such conditions produce what is known as a "white out." This is a phenomenon which renders the entire slope as one flat surface, and the unsuspecting skier may suddenly find himself dropping into a depression or hitting a "washboard" area or any number of other unpredictable slope changes. This can be somewhat disconcerting, if not downright dangerous. If the "white out" combines with a light snowfall, you may encounter another strange phenomenon known as vertigo, in which you simply are unable to determine your orientation. Unbelievable as it may seem, in such a situation one may not be able to gauge whether one is going downhill, uphill, or flat level. It is a strange sensation, and it is obvious the cautions one must take under these conditions.

If the over-50 skier heeds these few simple suggestions, and follows those made earlier, such as obtaining and maintaining the proper equipment, dressing appropriately for the weather conditions, taking lessons, and practice, practice, practicing on the beginners' slope, I can't think of any reason why his or her experience shouldn't parallel ours. It is likely such a skier will become as enthusiastic as the other millions who are skiing, including Pope John Paul II.

FOR MORE INFORMATION

No doubt, if you have read this far, your interest in downhill skiing has been aroused a little, at least. You will want to read more about various details of skiing than I've told you. There are a number of good books and magazines available and I've listed a sample of them below. A good place to go is your local public library or bookstore where you can select some materials to take home and read. If you do start skiing, no doubt you will want to subscribe to a ski magazine. It will give tips on improving your skiing, keep you up-to-date on new developments in ski equipment, show you where to ski, illustrate fashions in clothing, and stimulate your interest generally.

Books:
Auran, John H., and Jerry Winter. *The Ski Better Book: Skiing from the Edges Up.* New York, Dial, 1975. $4.95.
   A well-illustrated, practical guide to beginning skiing. Covers technique, equipment, psychology of skiing, and other helpful tips.
Casewit, Curtis W. *Complete Skier.* New York, Popular Library, 1974. $1.50.
   An inexpensive guide to inexpensive skiing. Useful for all skiers in choosing equipment, where to ski and stay in U.S. and Europe, and many more helpful suggestions to beat the high cost of skiing.
——. *Skiing Colorado.* Old Greenwich, Ct., The Chatham Press, $3.95.
Clein, Marvin I., and Joan-Marie Sanders. *Beginning Skiing.* Belmont, Ca., Wadsworth, 1968. $2.95.
   Written primarily for school physical education programs, this small book serves any beginner as well.
Guide to Colorado Ski Country USA. Colorado Ski Country USA, Denver, Co. Free.

Jensen, Clayne R., and Karl Tucker. *Skiing.* 2nd Ed. Dubuque, Ia., Wm. C. Brown, 1972. $2.50.

An inexpensive, yet good introduction for the beginning skier. Simple illustrations should prove helpful for home study following ski lessons.

Joubert, Georges. *Teach Yourself to Ski.* Aspen, Co., Aspen Ski Masters, 1972. $9.95 in gift box.

Well illustrated and simply explained in logical progression from beginning to advanced.

Killy, Jean-Claude. *133 Ski Lessons.* Chicago, Follett, 1975. $3.95.

Based on the author's syndicated newspaper series, this book brings together in orderly form instructional tips for beginners and experienced skiers.

Robinson, Gwen R. *Skiing: Conditioning & Techniques.* Palo Alto, Ca., Mayfield, 1974. $2.45.

Useful section on physical conditioning preparatory to skiing.

Styles, Merritt, and Robert D. O'Malley. *Ski at Any Age; Fitness Can Be Fun.* New York, Award House, 1971. $5.95.

Gives many examples of people over 50, and even to age 90, who ski. Includes case histories. Foreword by Lowell Thomas.

Magazines:

Ski. 7 times per year. P.O. Box 2798, Boulder, Co. 80321. $5.00 per year.

Skier. 8 times per year. Eastern Ski Association, 22 High Street, Brattleboro, Vt. 05301. $8.00 per year.

Skiing. Monthly. P.O. Box 2777, Boulder, Co. 80321. $7.00 per year.